Suddenly

"Man overboard! Man overboard!"

Ben rushed to the rail and saw a head protruding from the boiling sea. Without stopping to think, he reached over the side and grabbed the man by the hair of his head, until he could lay hold of his arm. With the help of the other passengers he got the half-drowned creature back on board. Ben immediately became a hero.

Ben Franklin
of
OLD PHILADELPHIA

By Margaret Cousins

Landmark Books®

Random House New York

www.randomhouse.com/kids

Cover engraving of Philadelphia Harbor c. 1835 courtesy of Mary Evans Picture Library.

Cover portrait of Benjamin Franklin by E. Fischer courtesy of Bettmann/CORBIS.

Library of Congress Cataloging-in-Publication Data
Cousins, Margaret. Ben Franklin of old Philadelphia. (Landmark books ; no. 10)
Includes index.
SUMMARY: A biography of the American who became known for his work as a printer,
author, inventor, and statesman.
1. Franklin, Benjamin, 1706–1790—Juvenile literature. 2. Statesmen—United States—
Biography—Juvenile literature. [1. Franklin, Benjamin, 1706–1790. 2. Statesmen.]
I. Title. E302.6.F8C74 1981 973.3'092'4 [B] [92] 81-806
ISBN 0-394-84928-0 AACR2

Printed in the United States of America 40 39 38 37 36 35 34 33 32 31

RANDOM HOUSE and colophon and LANDMARK BOOKS and colophon are registered
trademarks of Random House, Inc.

Contents

1

Water Baby

One freezing January Sunday in 1706, a gray-eyed baby boy was born to the wife of a soap- and candle-maker in Boston. The baby's parents would have been greatly surprised to know that their little son would do more different things in his lifetime than any other American of his century.

The very day he was born, the baby made a trip. In the arms of his father, he was carried across snow-covered Milk Street to the Old South Church, and with the icy water from the baptismal font, he was christened Benjamin Franklin.

Benjamin had a whole houseful of brothers and sisters. There were usually thirteen people at the Franklin table. While he was still very young, he learned to take care of himself and to keep out from underfoot. His mother was too busy cooking, washing, and sewing for her large family to keep an eagle eye on Ben, and his father was too busy making soap and candles.

Mr. Franklin sold his candles to the town of Boston for the night watch. Of course there were no streetlights in Boston then, any more than there were street numbers. In front of Ben's house there was a sign with a blue ball painted on it. People knew that you could buy soap and candles at the Sign of the Blue Ball. It was a busy place, and even a little boy had his chores and knew how to do things.

Everybody in Boston was busy in those days. It was a small town, the way we count things now, and it was located in a wild, new country. Each person, big and small, had to do his share, and if you didn't work, you might not eat. The government of the Colony of Massachusetts frowned on lazy people, and you could be whipped on your bare back if you did not choose to work.

Boston wasn't a particularly pretty or easygoing place, at that time, but it was a wonderful place to be a boy. The town was built around the harbor and the wharf, where sailing ships put in from England, bringing news and goods from the great world to the colonists. When a ship was sighted, the people swarmed onto the wharf and shouted in their excitement.

Narrow, winding streets, full of holes and bumps, climbed the low hills above the harbor. On each side of the streets rose square, unpainted houses, gray from the wind and rain and sun. Beyond, the great forests rolled away, nobody knew how far.

But for a boy, there were trees to climb, fish to catch, boats to sail, and canoes to paddle. There were the Commons, where Bostonians drove their cows to pasture; the marshes; the ponds; the river; and the sea. Boys built forts and stockades and played Indian, put together homemade boats and sailed the ponds as pirates, explored the woods and swam in the blue water.

Benjamin was a regular water baby and spent most of his time with his feet wet. He learned to swim almost as soon as he learned to walk, and he could sail a boat like a master. All summer long he splashed in the water like a little seal and his friends splashed after him. The names of those boys are now forgotten, but we can be sure that among them were Johns and Peters and Davids and Quincys and Obadiahs and Rogers.

Ben was the ringleader of the crowd, because his friends knew that in whatever place he was, something was sure to be going on. He could always think of something to do.

One day they were down at the salt marsh, fishing for minnows. Ben was standing there in his wet feet, waiting for a fish to bite, when he saw a crew of men beginning a building. They were working on a heap of stones. Right away he had an idea.

"Haloo," he called to his friends. "Why don't we build a wharf over here?"

"What for?" John wanted to know. He was the youngest and always asked silly questions.

"So we can stand on it to fish, Dunce Cap," said Ben. "We could tie our boats to it, too."

"Now, Ben," said Obadiah, "what dost thou think we can find to make a wharf with?" He was a Quaker boy, cautious and practical.

Ben jerked his fishpole toward the pile of stones. The workmen had dusted off their hands and gone home to supper.

"Rocks," he said.

"You mean move them over here?" It sounded like work.

"How else?" Ben said, throwing down his pole

and running toward the rock pile. The others followed him. For some reason they always wanted to do what he wanted to do.

Before you could say "Massachusetts," they were all tugging away at the big stones. Sweating and panting, they lugged them to the edge of the pond. There Ben drew a plan with a stick and bossed the job. Before nightfall the stones were fitted together to make a neat platform. Then, tired but happy, the boys went home.

They could hardly wait for morning so they could start fishing in comfort.

But this never happened.

When morning came, the men who had been putting up the building went back to their work, but their stones were missing. Each one had been moved over to the edge of the pond. Like angry hornets, the men went buzzing into Boston and made a great fuss to the fathers of the boys. The trouble began.

All over Boston, young lads were called on the carpet.

"What made you do a thing like that, Benjamin?" Josiah Franklin, a very honorable man, asked his son.

"We needed a wharf to fish from," Ben said. "Look what a good wharf we built, Pa!"

"But it isn't yours," Mr. Franklin pointed out sternly.

"Oh," said Ben.

By the time Ben and his friends had carried all the stones back to where they had come from, the boys had learned that rocks can be twice as heavy on the return trip. They had also learned to let other people's things alone. Everyone was hot and cross, and John fell down and skinned his shin.

"I told thee so!" Obadiah said to Ben.

For once Ben couldn't think of anything to say.

But nobody could stay angry at him for long. They might miss some fun! It wasn't long before he had thought up a way to make fins like those of a fish. With these strapped onto their ankles when they went swimming, the boys could streak through the water twice as fast, and leave an interesting trail of foam behind.

They never knew what Ben was going to do next. He was full of surprises. There was the time, for instance, when Ben brought the kite down to the pond. As he felt the wind pulling against it, he thought, It's almost strong enough to pull me! Then he thought, If I were in the water, I'll bet it would pull me!

The next time he went to the pond with his friends to swim, he took the kite.

"You can't fly a kite in the water!" Obadiah said.

"How do you know?" Ben asked.

He got the kite in the air and then took off his clothes and jumped in. Holding the kite string in his hand, he floated—and the kite, pushed by the wind, pulled him across the pond. William and Quincy, who were holding on to his clothes, were really amazed. They wanted to try it, too.

Ben was a hero for several days.

Benjamin loved the water all his life, and there was nothing about swimming that he did not learn to do. Years later when he was living in London, his fame as a swimmer spread and won him friends. He once put on an exhibition in the Thames River to the loud applause of people on the banks, and he taught several young Englishmen to swim as he did. When he founded a school in Philadelphia, he insisted that swimming be one of the studies—an unheard-of thing in those days.

Benjamin Franklin's ambition was to be a sailor, but that's one of the few things he never got to do.

2

Schoolboy

Life wasn't all swimming and summer and smooth sailing. The Boston winter was cruel and cold, with snow falling out of the sky like feathers from a pillow, and the wet, freezing winds blowing in from the sea. Frost coated the windowpanes, and long icicles hung by the outer walls of the houses. Never did the New World seem so wild and lonely as when winter came.

Ben did not mind it so much, because in the winter he had time to read. He could not remember when he had learned to read, but he loved it so

11

much that he would read anything. Even sermons! Nobody had many books when Benjamin was young, and people as poor as Ben's father had very few indeed. There were not many pictures in Mr. Franklin's books, which were all serious and dry and full of long, hard words. But Ben read them anyway, not once but over and over.

He would settle down by the hearth and read by the light of the fire, or by the crooked candles that came from the tallow shop. These were candles that had not been perfect enough to sell, and they were apt to flicker.

Of all the books he read, Ben liked *Pilgrim's Progress* best. It had a *story*.

When he was seven years old, he wrote a poem. This was so unusual that his father began to think about sending him to school. School was expensive and people like Mr. Franklin couldn't afford to educate all their children. But the next year Ben went to the Boston Grammar School.

At that time he was a middle-sized boy, chunky and strong, with a long head and a mop of curly hair. His eyes were large and brilliant and gray. In less than a year he worked his way to the head of the class, and he never had to be ashamed of his report card. Still, he did not think much of the Latin they tried to teach him at the Boston Grammar School.

"Why do I have to take Latin?" he complained. "Nobody speaks it anymore."

"You'll be sorry if you do not apply yourself, son," his father replied.

Ben may have been sorry but he never exactly admitted it. After he grew to be a man and learned to speak Spanish, Italian, and French, he looked at Latin again and saw that it was easy for him. It was his opinion that you should learn these languages first because they are simpler, and when you know them, Latin is easy. Before his life was over, he lived in France and had to speak French all the time. Some people said that his use of French grammar wasn't very good. They believed that if he had known Latin his French might have been better.

He didn't really have time to learn Latin when he was young, because he left the Boston Grammar School in less than a year, and went to Mr. Brownell's School for Writing and Arithmetic.

He learned to write a fair hand there, but he failed in arithmetic.

Nobody knows why Benjamin Franklin did so poorly in this subject. Mr. Brownell was supposed to be a very good teacher. It stands to reason that Ben's mind must have been on something else—probably *Pilgrim's Progress.*

He learned arithmetic later, however, digging it

out for himself, by himself, and became a wizard with figures. He even made up games with numbers, just for the fun of it. By this time he was no longer going to school but was working in his father's business, stirring the cauldrons of soap and pouring tallow into the candle molds. The greasy smell of the tallow was always in his nose and he hated tallow much worse than he hated arithmetic.

Ben hated it so much that after two years of trying to teach him the candle-maker's trade, his father began to look around for some other kind of work for his youngest son. He would take Ben by the hand and they would walk all over Boston, watching bricklayers and carpenters and braziers (brass workers) at their jobs. Mr. Franklin thought that in this way Ben might decide what sort of work he wanted to do.

Nothing happened, but from these tours of inspection Ben learned how to lay brick and do carpentry and machine work. In time he got to be quite handy around the house. But Ben grew more and more restless and Mr. Franklin grew more and more worried. Here was Ben, going on twelve, and he still hadn't decided what to do to earn a living!

"What do you *want* to do?" Mr. Franklin asked.

"Go to sea," his son said, promptly. "I want to be a sailor."

Most Boston boys wanted to go to sea, and Mr. Franklin knew how strong was the pull of the blue Atlantic, but he thought it a hard and unrewarding life. He could not bring himself to say yes to Benjamin. He was a patient man and a loving father, but he knew he had to act quickly.

Benjamin loved books. Why not let him learn how to make them? Mr. Franklin's son James had gone to England to study printing and had set up his own shop in Boston. That was the answer to the problem! Ben's father bound the boy over to his older brother as an apprentice and hoped for the best.

Ben was twelve years old. His schooling was over and his education had begun.

3

Apprentice

Ben had signed a paper, promising that until he was twenty-one years old he would work for his brother James as a helper. As his part of the bargain, James would provide Ben with food, a place to sleep, and lessons in printing.

Until he was twenty-one! That was nine long years away and only in the last year was Ben to receive wages. For eight years he would have no money at all. But the arrangement was not without its good points. Working in a print shop gave Ben a chance to meet the men who sold books in bookstores. Sometimes he could even borrow a book from a friendly bookseller at night and return it the next morning, being careful to keep it clean. After he had read several books of poetry in this way, he decided to write some poems.

He wrote a poem called "The Lighthouse Tragedy" about something that had really happened. It was the story of the drowning of a sea captain and his two daughters. James Franklin decided to print this poem in a little paper book. When it was finished, he sent Benjamin around town to sell the books. They sold very well, for people in those days did not have the sort of newspapers we have now and they liked to read the sad story of the lost captain.

With this success behind him, Ben then wrote a sailor's song (for his mind was always on going to sea) about the downfall of Teach, the pirate. It began:

> *Will you hear of a bloody battle,*
> *Lately fought upon the seas?*
> *It will make your ears rattle*
> *And your admiration cease.*
> *Have you heard of Teach, the Rover,*
> *And his knavery on the Main;*
> *How of gold he was a Lover,*
> *How he loved all ill-got Gain?*

Ben's father did not think much of this poem, which isn't very good, and he didn't like the idea of his son going from door to door, peddling his books. So he made fun of Ben. Had it not been for this, Benjamin might have become a poet instead of so many other things.

He did become a writer. But he didn't become a writer just by deciding he was going to be one. He went to a lot of trouble to learn how it was done. He would read a chapter in a book and then close the book and put it away. A few days later he would think about what he had read and rewrite it in his own words. He would then compare what he had written with the book he had read. His writing didn't sound as good as the book to him, and he realized it was because he didn't know enough words. So Ben decided to write in rhymes. In that way he would have to learn words that fitted the rhymes and yet had the same meanings as words that didn't rhyme. He would take several paragraphs of a book he was reading and turn them into verses. Later on, when he had pretty well forgotten the prose he had rhymed, he would take his verses and turn them back into the original prose. This was the way he learned new words.

While Ben was apprenticed to his brother James, he was kept pretty busy during the day. James was young and he was a hard master for his little brother. In fact, James had Ben running and fetching and carrying all day and was even harder on him than he might have been on an ordinary apprentice.

Ben had no time to read except at night after work or in the morning before work or on Sundays. He would read by candlelight, after everybody else had gone to bed, and by the first gray streaks of dawn in the mornings.

On Sunday, he was supposed to go to church, as was everybody else. Before Ben became an apprentice he had been obliged to go to church, for there wasn't any way out of it. His father made him go. After Ben went to work for James, he felt that he just didn't have time. Sunday was his best time for reading and learning new words and writing verses. So he stayed home and worked, but his conscience bothered him. This may have made him work harder, because he felt that it was his duty to be at church.

Ben Franklin learned to write by hard effort and with himself as his teacher, and it was one of the things he did best.

"Writing was of great use to me in my life, and was a principal means of my advancement," he said many years later.

Sometimes it is impossible for brothers to work together or to keep from fighting, especially when one brother is boss over the other. Ben and his brother James just couldn't get along. This made Ben's apprenticeship, which was such a change from the carefree days of his childhood, especially hard. Nor were James' other apprentices of much help, for they didn't seem very interesting. So Ben was lonely and missed his mother and sisters and his friends.

James wasn't married. Since he didn't have a home of his own, he boarded himself and his apprentices with a family he knew. Ben hated to go to the boarding house, where everybody nagged him because he had decided to stop eating meat. (He was always reading books and trying out things he read about, so when he read a book about the value of a vegetable diet, he decided to try it.) As meat was the principal feature of all meals in those days, everybody made fun of him, and James was embarrassed because his apprentice was attracting attention.

"I don't understand why you can't eat what everybody else eats," James said testily.

"I'm a vegetarian," Ben answered.

"You find yourself lucky that your master is able to provide you with meat," James declared.

"But I don't want it," Ben said.

"This is but another of your confounded poses," James cried, red as a beet.

"I will make a bargain with my master," Ben said sarcastically. "If you will give me weekly half the money you spend for my keep at the boarding house, I will feed myself and save you having to sit at the table with your inferior servant."

"Done," said James, who thought the bargain sounded too good to be true.

Ben thereupon became a cook. He looked up some recipes for cooking vegetables in the book he had read. Then, at the print shop, he started to boil up rice and potatoes and to make hasty pudding—a delicacy that was something like corn-meal mush and was usually eaten with molasses.

Although Ben had not planned to become his own cook, that is what he did. Nobody knows what kind of cook he was, but history doesn't record that his cooking made much of an impression. In fact, he said himself that he ate very light meals, sometimes no more than a handful of raisins, a biscuit or slice of bread, and a glass of water. At other times he dined on a tart bought at the pastry cook's. Hasty pudding probably turned out to be too much trouble!

The most important thing about the bargain

Ben made with his brother James was that he had time to read while the rest of the workers in the shop were away at their meals. The bargain also helped him to save a few cents. He would probably have starved before spending those few pennies James gave him. When he had a minute, he tried to think of ways to get out of his apprenticeship, and he knew that he would need money if he ever found a way.

When Ben was about fourteen years old, James Franklin decided to start a newspaper. It was the third newspaper to be founded in the city of Boston and was called the *New England Courant.* Some people thought it was pretty silly of James. After all, Boston already had two newspapers, the *Boston News-Letter* and the *Boston Gazette,* and what use was there for another one? James persevered in his rashness, however, and pretty soon the *New England Courant* made its appearance on the streets.

Ben was quite excited with the idea of the newspaper. He tried to hang around the editorial offices where James' friends gathered to discuss the articles that appeared in the paper and to talk about the ones they planned to write for it.

"Perhaps you could bring yourself to set a few sticks of type," James said to Ben one day, "instead of getting in the way of your elders. Your job is not to be concerned with the contents of the *Courant,* but with getting it in print."

Ben was shunted back to the composing room, where he not only set type for the paper but helped to print it. When he had finished that, he was ordered to put on his jacket and go shout out the headlines and sell it in the streets. While he was busy being a newsboy, his mind was also busy. How could he get something printed in the paper that people would read? When he heard James' friends praise the writing of some article or essay in the *Courant,* he ached to hear such praise of his own efforts.

He knew in his heart that James would never print anything he wrote. For one thing, he was still just a boy, and for another, James thought he was too smart for his own good already. But Ben thought of a way to get around that. He sat up late writing his thoughts out, and then he disguised his handwriting and copied his words over. He didn't put a name on his manuscript, and, running through the dark street, late at night, he pushed it under the door of the printing house where he spent his days at hard labor.

The next morning when James unlocked the door, he found the manuscript.

"What's this?" James said, looking over the neat

script and searching for the author's name. "It seems to be anonymous!"

"I don't suppose it can be any good, if the writer didn't put his name to it," said Ben, offhandedly.

"On the contrary," said James, who could never bring himself to agree with Ben on any subject. "It's quite interesting. I think I'll show it to the others."

When James' friends dropped in, as they always did, James displayed the manuscript as an evidence of the attention the *Courant* was beginning to attract.

While Ben lurked in the doorway, the manuscript was read aloud. Everybody thought it was fine, and they all tried to guess the name of the author. Ben wanted to shout: "I wrote it!"

Ben wrote many of these secret, anonymous pieces, and when his brother's friends continued to praise them, his vanity finally overcame him and he admitted that he was the author. This did not set very well with James, as you can imagine. His friends began to include young Ben in their circle, and that irked James. Besides, he did not like the idea of having been fooled by his little brother. He thought all this attention made Benjamin vainer than he already was, and the brothers began to quarrel in earnest.

Their disputes usually wound up before their

father for settlement. Although the elder Franklin often sided with his younger son, he still impressed on Benjamin the importance of James' position as master and Ben's need for humility as an apprentice.

James took his position seriously. He was a hotheaded man with a high temper, and when Benjamin displeased him, he set on him and beat him. Ben resented this fiercely, largely because the punishments seemed to him too big to fit the crimes. He despised these beatings and resented James' right to give them to him.

Ben had an independent spirit and did not believe that one man ought to be allowed to have complete power over another. He felt the same way all his life, and he said that his hatred and distrust of dictators sprang from his miseries as an apprentice to his own brother.

James' hot-headed nature eventually got him into trouble with the Massachusetts Assembly. One of the articles he printed in the newspaper angered the members of the Assembly, and James was hauled off to jail for a month, to cool his head and his heels.

Ben, who had been angry at his brother for years, now transferred his anger to the Assembly. He thought that newspapers ought to be allowed to say what they thought. While James was in jail, Ben edited the *New England Courant*, and every time he had a chance, he made a few slighting remarks about the Assembly of Massachusetts.

Because of this loyalty, James felt more kindly toward Ben. Of course, this change in feeling may also have been due to the fact that James was in prison and didn't see much of Benjamin! At any rate, when the older brother had served his sentence and came home with an order from the Assembly that he, James Franklin, was no longer allowed to print the *New England Courant*, he decided to print the paper in Ben's name.

In order to make this transfer, James returned to Ben his apprentice papers, with a full discharge written on the back of them. This was necessary to show that Ben was a free man, and able to publish a newspaper. But privately, James presented his brother with a new set of papers for the remainder of his apprenticeship period. These papers were exactly like the old ones. James wanted to have his cake and eat it too.

Ben signed the new papers and went on publishing the *Courant*, but James, without realizing it, had left Ben a loophole. Nobody else knew anything about the second set of apprentice papers, and the situation with the *Courant* made it impossible for James to admit that he held them.

The next time James struck Ben in a quarrel, Ben resisted him and pointed out that he was a free man.

James was in a rage. However, he could not make public his secret agreement with his brother without serious consequences to himself. If the Massachusetts Assembly discovered what had happened, he might find himself back in jail.

"This is fine payment for all I have done for you," James shouted.

"I suppose being beaten around the head is good training for the printing business," Ben returned.

"I do not think you will long be in the printing business," James said coldly. "I will see to that."

"It would be a pity to waste so many years of my affectionate brother's instruction," Ben said. "There is very little about a print shop I have not learned in this unhappy place."

"I would be ashamed to have any other master know how little discipline you have learned," said James.

He then made it his business to call on every printer in Boston and tell them the story, so that nobody would give Ben a job.

Ben did not know which way to turn. His personal attacks on the Massachusetts Assembly had not made him popular in Boston. His failure to go to church and some of the things he had said about religion had resulted in people looking at him with horror and calling him an infidel. His father was hurt and disgusted with him.

Ben knew that he would have to run away from Boston if he was ever to get started, and that's what he did next.

4

Runaway

One gloomy October morning, Benjamin crept out of the house before dawn and got aboard a ship in the Boston Harbor, bound for New York. His one friend, John Collins, had arranged with the captain of the vessel to take him aboard secretly. Ben knew that if he tried to leave James' printing house openly, the means of stopping him would be found. He had sold his dearly beloved and hard-earned books to get money for the passage, and his heart was heavy when he saw the widening path of water separate him from his home.

The wind was fair and the vessel sailed rapidly. After a trip of three days—it took three days in those times to get from Boston to New York—he found himself alone in a strange town. He was seventeen years old, had only a few pennies, and did not know anybody.

He applied at once to William Bradford, the only printer in New York (which was hardly more than a village in those days), but Mr. Bradford said that business was terrible. Furthermore, he already had too much help.

"My son in Philadelphia has lately lost his principal hand; if you go thither, I believe he may employ you," Mr. Bradford added. Benjamin decided at once to go, since he had to have a job.

It was a hundred miles to Philadelphia, and there were no railroads at that time. Ben hurried down to the waterfront and boarded a ferryboat that was bound for Perth Amboy, a town in what would someday be the state of New Jersey.

The ferry looked rickety, with sails that were old and rotten. It was crowded with people who jostled Ben at the railing as they set out. The sky was gray and overcast and tongues of lightning licked out of the low-hanging clouds. As the boat pulled away from the ferry slip, the rising wind began to drive it out to sea instead of toward

Perth Amboy. Ben, with his knowledge of boats, saw the captain struggling with the wheel of the bucking little craft and he felt very nervous.

Soon the storm broke over the decks in full fury. Rain poured out of the heavens like the downspouts of a gutter. The wind howled around the ship and began to pick at the rotting sails. With a great splitting sound, these at last gave way before its force. The cries of the drenched passengers, as they tried to find cover, mingled with the noise of tearing canvas. Suddenly there was a sharper cry.

"Man overboard! Man overboard!"

Ben rushed to the rail and saw a head protruding from the boiling sea. Without stopping to think, he reached over the side and grabbed the man by his hair. Pulling and tugging, Ben hauled him up out of the water by the hair of his head, until he could lay hold of his arm. With the help of the other passengers he got the half-drowned creature back on board. Ben immediately became a hero.

"Land, ho!" shouted the boatmen. Sure enough, straight ahead of them was a rocky shore—but it was nowhere near Perth Amboy. It was the coast of Long Island.

The passengers sighed with relief, but the ferry captain did not share this general rejoicing. It took all his time to keep his ferry from being bashed up on the rocks. The wind had died a little but the surf was rolling high and wide. The great waves caught the little boat in their troughs and spun it around.

The passengers looked eagerly at the land, almost within reach, but they never got to it. All night long the waves and spray dashed over the decks while the boatmen and passengers cowered in the scuttle (a small opening in the deck) of the boat, trying to sleep. But they couldn't sleep. They were too thirsty and hungry. Thirty hours, without food or water, went by before the storm blew itself out and they finally made port in Perth Amboy.

If you look at a map you will see that Perth Amboy is still a long way from Philadelphia, and young Mr. Franklin discovered that the next leg of his journey would be by foot. He had to walk fifty miles to Burlington to get another boat to take him to Philadelphia. To make matters worse, he was sick with a fever from exposure in the ferryboat, and he had too little money to buy medicine. He just drank a lot of cold water and went to bed.

The next morning he got up and set out. It was pouring rain and by noon he was soaking wet and very tired. He wished he had never left home. Unable to walk another step, he stayed at a poor inn that afternoon and night, but he was afraid to linger there. He was dirty and bedraggled and his clothes were a sight to see. He had left his luggage in New York and was wearing his work clothes. His extra socks and shirts were stuffed in all his pockets. Everybody at the inn took him for a runaway servant, and he was afraid he would be captured and clapped in jail.

Ben spent a restless night on a miserable bed. He was still weak from his sickness, and the weather was cold and raw. Most of all, he feared the tread on the stairs that might prove to be an officer, ready to throw him in jail. The fact that he wasn't a runaway servant, that he had done nothing to deserve jail, wouldn't have made much difference to the king's men in those days. Ben was friendless and alone and he didn't want to wind up back in Boston after he had gone to so much trouble to run away.

As soon as it was daylight, he got up, gathered together his few belongings, which he once more stuffed in his pockets, and hiked on toward Philadelphia. It was Saturday and when he finally arrived in Burlington, the streets were full of people trading.

"Gingerbread! Hot gingerbread," he heard somebody say.

Ben suddenly felt starved. "I'll buy some of that," he said, and looked in his thin purse for a coin.

The rosy old lady who was selling the gingerbread smiled at him and gave him a large piece. He looked so young.

Ben grabbed his gingerbread and hurried on toward the wharf.

"I want to take a boat for Philadelphia," he said to a man on the pier. "Where would I find it?"

"Ye won't find her anywhere today, boy," the man said. "She sailed an hour ago."

Ben sighed. Hard luck seemed to be on his trail. "When, then?" he asked.

"Not afore Tuesday," said the man. "She must make the return trip and rest up."

Never had Ben been more downcast. He did not know how he would live until Tuesday, for his money was almost gone. "Isn't anybody going to Philadelphia?" Ben pleaded. "I would make a hand."

"Not as I know," the man said. "Not till Tuesday."

Ben turned and walked sadly back up the street. He was almost at the end of his rope.

"Is your hurrying over?" an old voice said, and he saw the gingerbread lady watching him.

"The boat has sailed," Ben told her. "And I can't get another until Tuesday. I don't know what to do."

36

"Wait for Tuesday," she said.

"But I have no place to stay."

"You seem a likely lad," she said. "You could stay with me if you could put up with a simple home."

"But I have no money," Ben said. "I couldn't pay you."

"There was no word about money mentioned," said the old lady. "I was inviting a guest."

. Ben's eyes felt damp with tears, though he was a big boy. It seemed to him a long time since anybody had shown him a true kindness. He was so grateful to the old lady that he felt like kissing her.

"You don't know me," Ben said. "How can you take a stranger under your roof? I might be a criminal."

"Might you not," she said. "But I know enough of people to know you are only a boy, unhappy and lost, and in need of a lodging until Tuesday."

"Lead on, dear lady," Ben said. "You have told my fortune and you have a guest."

She gave him another piece of gingerbread and took him home with her.

That evening, while Ben was walking along the river's edge, a boat headed for Philadelphia came by.

"Ahoy!" Ben called. "Are you bound for Philadelphia?"

"Aye," one of the sailors called back across the water.

"Would you take on a good hand?" Benjamin asked.

"We're sore crowded already," the sailor said, "but I don't know as one more would make a difference."

The captain was consulted and they took him on. Later they were glad of it.

There was no wind for the sails that night and the crew rowed all the way. Ben had been rowing since he was a small boy, and he made a good hand at the oars. But the captain got lost and could not find Philadelphia. The party finally landed in a little creek. There the men crawled out, tore down the rails of a nearby fence, and made a fire, for they were all about to freeze.

The next morning they poled out of the creek and saw the spires of Philadelphia.

"Thar she blows!" cried one of the boatmen, and Franklin looked for the first time on his new home.

He did not feel very inspired by the sight. It was Sunday morning and he was worn out from walking, rowing, and not sleeping. He had only a dollar in his pocket, and nowhere to go. He went gawking up the street until he saw a boy eating a piece of bread. Ben asked where he could buy some, and the boy directed him to the baker.

"I'll have a biscuit," Ben said to the baker, reaching for his three-pence coin.

"We have no such here," said the baker. "What is a biscuit?"

"In Boston we have biscuits," Ben said.

"This is Philadelphia," said the baker.

"Then give me a three-penny loaf," Ben said. "I am hungry."

"That may well be," said the baker, "but of three-penny loaves I have none."

"Then give me three penny'worth of *any* kind of bread," said Ben, who was getting hungrier and angrier by the minute.

The baker handed him three enormous puffy rolls. Ben was flabbergasted. He didn't know what to do with them. There was no room in his pockets, which were already full of his spare socks and shirts. He wanted to hand back two of them and ask for his two pennies, but he didn't have the courage. He finally stowed one roll under each arm and walked down the street munching on the other.

As he trudged down Market Street toward Fourth, he passed a pretty girl standing in her father's doorway. He looked so silly, loaded down with bread, that she laughed at him. He felt like a fool and it made him furious to be laughed at by a girl, especially such a pretty one. He would have liked to give her a piece of his mind but his mouth was full of bread.

He didn't know it at the time, but this was his first meeting with his future wife. The girl's name was Deborah Read, and a few years later he married her.

5
Printer

Ben Franklin worked at many things and he was a good businessman, but he always thought of himself as a printer. He had come to Philadelphia to be a printer and no other kind of work entered his head.

After giving away his two extra rolls to an old lady and a boy who looked hungrier than he was, he followed the well-dressed crowds in the Philadelphia streets. It turned out that the crowd was going to the Quaker Meeting House.

Ben went in and sat down to think, but he fell fast

asleep. He didn't wake up until somebody tapped him on the shoulder and told him church was over. Deciding that he had better catch up with his sleep before looking for work, he rented a room and slept for a long time. Then he hunted up Andrew Bradford, who was William Bradford's son.

"I just hired a hand," Mr. Bradford said, and this made Ben very sad. It seemed to him he was always just missing the boat.

"Maybe Samuel Keimer could use you," Mr. Bradford said, looking Ben over and liking what he saw.

They went to see Mr. Keimer, another printer.

"Neighbor," said Mr. Bradford to Samuel Keimer, "I have brought to see you a young man of your business; perhaps you may want such a one."

Mr. Keimer fingered his long beard and looked at Ben, whose looks had now been considerably improved by washing and clean clothes. He finally decided to give the boy a job, and Ben at last began to earn real wages.

During that first winter in Philadelphia, Benjamin had a wonderful time. He was a free man, with money jingling in his pockets. His father wasn't standing over him telling him what to do, and his brother James wasn't bullying him and giving him whippings.

At that time Philadelphia was the largest town in the American colonies—bigger than Boston and New York put together—and its people were the best educated and the richest. While it was not much like a big city, as we think of big cities today, it was the "city" of the colonies. Though Boston was a huddle of weathered gray houses, rising above the blue harbor, Philadelphia was a town of bright colors. Most of the shop fronts were painted red, blue, green, or yellow, and the big swinging signs in front of them were brilliant with paint and gilt. The carriages that bounced over the muddy, rutted streets were also gay with paint.

The people of Philadelphia wore bright colors and had a taste for fine clothes, although some of the Quakers still wore gray from head to foot. However, the rich Quakers followed the fashion and wore silks, satins, and velvets in all the colors of the rainbow, along with wigs and jewelry. The ladies dressed in elaborate clothes, too, and with their high hairdos, they looked very pretty.

Philadelphians loved to have company and parties; they enjoyed getting together to talk and sing and eat. People had fewer places of amusement to visit in those days, so they stayed at home and did a lot of talking. Conversation was important.

Ben Franklin loved to talk, too, and he read so

many books that he had a good deal to talk about. In Philadelphia he met young people his own age who were interested in reading and in other things that he enjoyed. He began to make friends— something that was never very hard for Ben, and something that he continued to do until the end of his life.

His boss, Mr. Keimer, arranged for him to have room and board at the house of Mr. Read. This man was the father of Deborah Read, the girl who had laughed to see young Franklin carrying his puffy rolls down the street.

So began Ben's happy days in Philadelphia, the city that was to become his real hometown for the rest of his life, though he was to live all over the world.

Probably there is no year in anybody's life like that first year away from home, when one has ceased to be a boy and has become a young man, making one's own money and choosing one's own companions. Ben's last days in Boston had been so unhappy that he tried to forget Boston as much as possible. For one thing, he was afraid that James might be able to think up some scheme to get him back to his dreary apprenticeship. For that reason, he kept his whereabouts secret and wrote nobody in Boston except John Collins, who had sworn not to tell.

However, word of Benjamin's presence in Philadelphia got around and traveled as far south as Newcastle, Delaware. There, Captain Robert Holmes, the husband of one of Ben's sisters, and the master of a sailing ship that traded between Boston and Delaware, got wind of the news. At once he wrote his young brother-in-law a troubled letter, asking him to return home. Everybody was upset and worried, he said, over the prodigal son.

Ben was still smarting under the memory of James' beatings and the fact that he had kept him from getting a job in Boston. He answered Captain Holmes with a letter in which he said as much. He added a few other details concerning his reasons for leaving Boston.

Now, Ben Franklin was a great letter writer. Even when he wasn't quite grown-up, he wrote the sort of letter that made a deep impression on anybody who read it.

When Ben's letter was delivered, Captain Holmes happened to be in conversation with the English Governor of Pennsylvania, Sir William Keith.

"My young relative is a man of spirit," Captain Holmes said, when he had finished the letter. "Runaway though he be!"

"Runaway?" Sir William said.

Captain Holmes told him the story and passed

over the letter. "He states his reasons in this," he said.

"He has a pretty wit," Sir William said, "and a good head on his shoulders. Say to him that he should come and see me."

Sir William was feeling generous. He advised Captain Holmes that such a smart boy ought to open his own print shop in Philadelphia and do business with the Colony of Pennsylvania. Moreover, Sir William, who was a man of action, didn't let the matter drop. He called at Samuel Keimer's print shop in Philadelphia.

You can imagine what a fuss this stirred up in the neighborhood and the print shop, to have the Governor of the Colony of Pennsylvania calling. Everybody scurried about and Mr. Keimer, who did not know why he had received the honor of this visit, bowed low and welcomed the governor, who was accompanied by a friend from Delaware, Colonel French.

"I have come to inquire for the printer Franklin," Sir William said. "Please to bring him here."

Mr. Keimer's eyes nearly popped out. Ben said later that he stared like a poisoned pig.

When the eighteen-year-old youth was hauled before him, the governor treated him with respect and flattery and invited him to go down to the

tavern on the corner. There they had some refreshments and a talk.

"You are a bright lad," Sir William said. "Why do
you not go into business for yourself and make
your fortune? We have need in the government for
good printing. I would see to it that you got
orders."

"You do me a great honor," Ben said. "But, sir, I
have no money for the purchase of type or presses."

"Perhaps your father would lend you the means
to get started," the governor said.

Ben did not like to say that he had run away
from home and broken his apprenticeship con-
tract. Also, he did not feel very optimistic about
the chances of Josiah Franklin's setting him up in
business in Philadelphia, especially since his
father didn't know he was there.

"I do not know what my father would say to
this," he said after a moment.

"I will write him a letter," said Sir William, "and
you can take it to Boston and urge him."

"All right," Ben said. "It is more than good of you."

"Perhaps it would be wise to make no mention
of this," Sir William Keith said. "Or your employer
may light a fire under you."

Ben went back to work with his thrilling secret.
Not long after, Governor Keith sent him a letter

addressed to Josiah Franklin. It was full of compliments about Ben and urged the boy's father to give him the money to go into business.

So only seven months after he had left Boston under a dark cloud, Benjamin Franklin went back. This time he was dressed in fine new clothes from head to foot and his pockets were full of silver money. He was carrying a watch and, more important, a letter from the Governor of the Colony of Pennsylvania.

His family had heard no news of him since he had left (his brother-in-law, Captain Holmes, was still at sea), and they were really surprised to see him and to notice the fine figure he cut. They all made him welcome except James.

Ben could not wait to get over to James' print shop to show off his wealth. All his former co-workers crowded around him to finger his new suit and to ask him about Philadelphia, but James sulked alone and would take no part.

"It's a wonderful place," Ben said. "My life there is most happy and I cannot wait to return."

"I doubt not they miss you," James said from his corner. "Perhaps the sooner you return the better."

"The society is very agreeable in Pennsylvania," Ben said. "Which is more than I can say of this place!"

"It must be very rich there," said one of the apprentices. "I suppose all have money."

"Oh, yes, indeed," said Ben and took out a handful of silver. The apprentices' eyes popped. In Boston they used paper money and rarely saw silver.

"I would like to stand treat for a round of refreshments," Ben said, and threw a coin down with a grand air.

James gritted his teeth, but all the apprentices and printers accepted with enthusiasm.

"Well, I must be going on," Ben said. "I have personal business." He took his watch out of his pocket and looked at the time.

Now a watch was a rare thing in the colonies in those days and there probably wasn't a man in the place who had hope of ever owning one. They stared at it in amazement and wanted to handle the beautiful toy.

This was the last straw for James. He never forgave Ben for showing off in front of his workmen. When their mother tried to bring the two brothers together to make peace in the family, James said that Ben had insulted him beyond forgiveness. But Ben felt that he had done nothing more than repay the beatings and the bad treatment he had received from James.

Ben showed the letter from Sir William Keith to his father, and Josiah came as near to snorting as a man of his dignity could come.

"What sort of man is this who thinks of setting up a boy in business?" he demanded. "You are still three years short of being grown!"

"Well, he's the governor!" Ben said in a small voice. "He ought to know."

Josiah Franklin, like most American colonists, was an independent man who was not bowled over by titles.

"I am your father," he stated. "I know you better than he does."

"Yes, sir," said Ben, coming down to earth off his rosy cloud.

"Wait until you have had more experience," his father counseled. "You are too young for the responsibilities of handling the money of other people."

Ben saw that his father was not going to fall in with the governor's scheme, so he got ready to go back to Philadelphia. His father did not protest this move, but he gave him a lecture on how to behave and save his money. He wrote Sir William Keith that he felt his son was too young and inexperienced to own his own business.

"Your father is too careful," Sir William said to

Ben when he had read this letter. "I am of the opinion that age has little to do with such matters. But do not fret. I am determined to have a good printer in this colony and I will set you up myself!"

Sir William then asked Ben to make a list of what he would need and suggested that he make a voyage to England to purchase his printing equipment.

"I will supply you with funds," said the governor, "and you may repay me from your profits."

Ben thought this was fine, and learned too late that the governor did not have the money to set him up. Sir William was a kind gentleman who wanted everybody to like him, and, since he didn't have much money, he was fond of making promises that he couldn't keep.

Ben was already on a ship going to England to buy a printing press and type when he found that the governor had failed to send him the letters and the money he would need. He did not have enough money to get passage back to America, so he went to work in a print shop in England. Perhaps it is an ill wind that blows nobody good, for when he finally did get home, he knew more about printing than anybody else in America. He had learned it the hard way.

He worked in London printing shops for a year

and a half. Then, just as he was getting very home-sick, a Philadelphia merchant named Denham offered him a job in a new store he was opening on Water Street in Philadelphia. Ben quickly accepted the offer and Mr. Denham advanced him the money for his passage. He worked in Mr. Denham's general store in Philadelphia, where he learned how to sell goods and keep books, but before long Mr. Denham and Ben both got very sick with pleurisy and Mr. Denham died. Penniless again, Franklin applied to Mr. Keimer for his old job.

From this job, Ben got fired. Mr. Keimer had hired Ben to train a group of men, but as soon as the men were trained, he planned to get rid of Ben. The employer was just using him for his own profit, because Ben was a master of the art of printing.

One day there was a loud noise in the street under the print-shop window and Ben, who was supposed to be working, stuck his head out to see what was going on. He saw Mr. Keimer, and Mr. Keimer saw him.

"Mind your own business!" Mr. Keimer shouted to Ben, and came racing upstairs to reprimand his employee for leaving his work. At the same time he gave young Franklin notice that he was to stop working for him in a few weeks.

52

"I will leave this instant," Ben cried proudly. Jamming his hat on his head, he walked out of the shop without taking any of his belongings.

That night Hugh Meredith, one of the young men who were apprenticed to Samuel Keimer, gathered up Ben's things and delivered them to him. Ben was very discouraged and was beginning to think about going back to Boston and trying to start over. Hugh hated to think of losing Ben as a friend, so he said, "Why don't we go into the printing business together?"

"But I have no money," said Ben with a sigh. It seemed to him that he had suffered from the lack of money since he was old enough to remember.

"Well, Pa has," said Meredith. "Maybe he would lend it to us. I'll put in the money and you put in the brains."

Ben could hardly refuse this flattering offer, and Hugh asked his father. When the elder Meredith agreed, orders for a printing press and type were sent off to England on the next boat. But ships to England took a long time in those days. It would be months before they could get started.

In the meantime, Mr. Keimer, who had been given a chance to print some paper money for the Colony of New Jersey, asked Ben to forgive and forget and come back to work. Hugh Meredith was delighted because he still had several months of apprenticeship there, and, of course, Ben was idle and needed the money. So, for the third time Ben went to work for Samuel Keimer.

One of the important things Ben did in this job was to make the first copperplate printing press in America. He designed the bills for New Jersey and cut ornaments to decorate them. He and Samuel Keimer journeyed up to Burlington, where the New Jersey Assembly held its meetings, and there they printed New Jersey's paper money. The Assembly was very pleased with it. Here Franklin made many more friends. The members of the Assembly soon began to take him home to dinner and introduce him to their wives and daughters.

Not long after this job was finished, the printing press and type that Mr. Meredith had ordered from England arrived in Philadelphia. As quickly as possible, Hugh and Ben settled with Mr. Keimer, rented a house on Market Street, and opened up their own shop. Their first customer was a farmer who was wandering around the streets looking for a place to get some printing done. He was brought into the new shop and he spent five shillings! Ben said this was the most wonderful money he ever earned.

Meredith and Franklin had two competitors in Philadelphia—Andrew Bradford, who did all the government printing, and Mr. Keimer, their former employer. After Franklin and Meredith left him, Mr. Keimer got deeply into debt and became even more quarrelsome. Finally he was forced to sell his newspaper, and eventually his printing business. The latter was bought by a young man who had learned the printing business from Ben.

Ben himself bought the newspaper, which he called the *Pennsylvania Gazette*. In addition to being printer of the newspaper, he was also its writer, reporter, editor, and advertising salesman. One of the important things he did was to print local news about people who lived in Pennsylvania. This was rather unusual for a newspaper in those days. He wrote or rewrote all the news. He wrote letters to himself as the editor, under assumed names, and then answered them himself. He wrote funny things and he even wrote the advertisements. He began to get more and more readers and more and more advertisers.

As the *Gazette* became important, his rival in the printing business, Andrew Bradford, began to worry that Ben might take all his business away. Mr. Bradford was postmaster and he refused to permit post-office carriers to deliver Ben's newspaper. Ben thought this was pretty unfair and he did not hesitate to make a secret agreement with the mail carriers and pay them for their trouble.

Out of Ben Franklin's *Pennsylvania Gazette* came the *Saturday Evening Post*, which you can still buy today.

The next thing Ben did was to print, without cost, some speeches from the Assembly. His printing was so much better than Andrew Bradford's that the members of the Assembly couldn't help noticing the fact. So only two years after he and Hugh Meredith had set up their business on a shoestring, Franklin became printer for the Colony of Pennsylvania. Not long after that, Ben bought out Hugh Meredith, with borrowed money. Saddled with heavy debts, Ben struck out on his own.

Nobody knows how hard Ben had to work then, but he said of himself: "I never went a-fishing or shooting." He even found very little time to read his precious books. He used to buy the paper for his newspaper and trundle it through the streets on a wheelbarrow, so he was also a truckman. He opened a stationery store, so he was also a merchant.

When Ben Franklin was twenty-six years old, he printed the first copy of *Poor Richard's Almanac*. People still talk about *Poor Richard* today, and when you hear such proverbs as "A stitch in time saves nine" or "Little strokes fell great oaks," you can remember that they were first written that way in *Poor Richard's Almanac,* by Benjamin Franklin.

When Ben first brought out *Poor Richard's Almanac,* under the name of Richard Saunders, almanacs were the most popular of all books in colonial America. In almost every home—even those that had no other printed matter—there was usually an almanac to be found.

Almanacs were the weather bureaus of those days, claiming to forecast the weather and setting down the changes of the moon and the times of the tides. They also contained riddles, jokes, little poems, proverbs, odd facts, recipes, tips on planting the garden, superstitions, and a hodgepodge of all kinds of things. Many children learned to read from almanacs, and in their margins people kept diaries and other notes, for few had paper. An almanac was necessary to a household.

Ben didn't invent the almanac. Many people, including Bradford and Keimer, had printed them before him. Almanacs came out in the fall, foretelling the weather for the following year. *Poor Richard* was late. The first issue came off the presses on December 19, 1732, and was sold at five pence per copy. Before New Year's rolled around, it had gone into three printings and passed all its established rivals in the almanac field. This was due largely to Benjamin Franklin's writing and thinking.

Poor Richard prospered and so did Ben. He paid off his debts and became rich and successful. Every year *Poor Richard's Almanac* sold more and more copies until each year ten thousand people wanted to know what *Poor Richard* had to say.

As *Poor Richard's Almanac* became famous, so did the *Pennsylvania Gazette*. Eventually it grew to be the most important newspaper in the colonies, and Ben hired riders on horseback to deliver it in order to get the news to the people quickly.

With all the other things that Ben Franklin did, he continued to think of himself as a printer. When he wrote his will, after he had been Ambassador to the Court of France, he began it: "I, Benjamin Franklin, printer. . . ."

Printing was his trade.

6

Good Citizen

As soon as Ben Franklin's business began to make money, he found that he had time to notice things that needed to be done for the good of everybody. By now he had married his sweetheart, Deborah, and settled down with Philadelphia as his home.

Like most printers in those days, he lived over his shop in the busy marketplace, and his house was full of his children, his relatives, the people who worked for him in the print shop, servants, and occasionally friends who came to stay. It was a happy household, but one that was very hard to keep clean.

Ben saw how the people of Philadelphia, coming to the marketplace, had to wade through mud and dirt to buy their groceries. Finally he had a foot-path put down the middle of the market. Then, by talking and writing editorials for the *Gazette*, he got the street paved with stones so that people could get around with dry feet. This kept a great amount of dirt from being tracked into the houses.

No sooner had he managed this than he noticed that when a carriage came down the street it shook off mud onto the pavement. This mud was then carried into homes on the people's feet. Franklin looked around until he found a poor man who was willing to sweep the street twice a week if he was paid sixpence by each of the households along the way. Franklin wrote a paper about this and sent it around to all his neighbors. Then he went out and asked them to subscribe sixpence a week for this purpose. This was probably the first time there was any street sweeping in America.

Not satisfied with just *sweeping* the streets, Ben hired an old lady who would not only sweep the street, but collect the refuse and dust in a heap to be washed down the gutter. Ben then decided that horse-drawn carts should be used to take away the mud and dirt. This was the forerunner of sanitation departments and garbage collectors, now so familiar and important to us all.

It was Ben Franklin who drew the first bill for the paving of the streets in Philadelphia. Inspired by the spic-and-span marketplace, Philadelphians willingly paid a tax for the purpose.

Ben did not start the lighting of streets in Philadelphia, but he improved it. He invented a new kind of street lamp that had four small panes instead of one round globe. These square lamps, which you can still see in some cities, permitted the smoke from the flame to rise and the lamp to stay clean and to shine brightly. Also, such lamps were more easily repaired. If one pane of glass in these four-sided globes was broken, it was not necessary to throw away the lamp, but only to replace one pane of glass.

It is hard for us to imagine how frightening fires were in those days, when there were no water systems or fire engines or even hook-and-ladder wagons (as in Boston) to put them out. If something caught fire in Philadelphia when Franklin was a young man, it just burned up—but not before it had set fire to everything else in the neighborhood.

This made Ben very nervous. He wrote a letter to himself, signed it "An *Old* Citizen," and published it in his paper. In the letter he laid down a number of rules for fire prevention. One rule said people oughtn't to carry hot coals from one room to another unless the warming pan was shut tight!

He then suggested that Philadelphia take a leaf out of Boston's book and organize a volunteer fire company. Inspired by the letters that he wrote to himself on this subject, Franklin organized the Union Fire Company. There were thirty members, and each had his own leather bucket and strong canvas bag for carrying goods. Many of these fire companies were later formed because such a great number of men joined the first one that it overflowed and got too big.

Soon Philadelphia had a network of volunteer fire companies and was the safest city in the world as far as fires went. Almost every man in Philadelphia who owned property bought himself a leather bucket and joined a fire company. These companies charged a small fine when the members were absent from the monthly meeting, and the fines were used to buy hook-and-ladder wagons.

Ben wasn't satisfied with the police department in Philadelphia, either. When he walked the rounds of the city watch one night just for amusement, it seemed to him that most of the watchers were more interested in the rum bottle than they were in protecting the people. Ben suggested that it would be better to hire regular policemen and pay them a salary than to depend on the system of elected constables. Sometimes these constables hired helpers who struck Ben as being not much better than the thieves and bandits they were supposedly trying to catch.

From his earliest days, Ben had been a book-lover, and he knew how hard it was for most people to get books. After thinking about this, he hit upon a plan that would make more books available to those who liked to read. Ben had organized a club named the Junto, where all the members shared their books. These were lent and borrowed and passed around until each book had been read by everybody in the club. But then the members wanted more books to read.

Ben suggested that each member of the Junto contribute a sum of money to buy books and invite anybody else in Philadelphia who wanted to read to do the same. Fifty people signed up and they ordered a long list of books from London. When the books came, they were set up in the Junto's clubroom, where anybody could drop in and read them, but only members could take them home. This was the beginning of circulating libraries in America.

The first library was really circulating, for not only did the books move from hand to hand, but they were kept in different places, too. Sometimes they were at the Junto clubroom, other times they were at the houses of various members who served as librarians, free of charge. Ben printed a catalogue of the books and gave it away to the members of the library.

Ben, in addition to being a real bookworm, was a letter writer who has had few equals. He loved letters and it used to bother him that it took so long to get a reply to letters he wrote in America. This led him to look into the postal system and try to find out why the mails were so poor.

His interest in mail delivery resulted in his being made controller of postal matters in Philadelphia, where he reorganized the whole system of bookkeeping and mail service. He arranged to have three mails a week between Philadelphia and New York instead of just one. When he had made it possible to send a letter to Boston from Philadelphia and get back an answer in three weeks, he felt very triumphant.

Franklin rode over all the postal routes in colonial America on horseback—a long, rough ride— helping the local postmasters straighten out their accounts and giving them advice on their problems. In four years he put the colonial post-office system on a paying basis and soon the colonies were sending profits to England.

When the Continental Congress met, after the colonies had begun to fight for their freedom, Ben was elected postmaster general. His salary of a thousand dollars a year he donated to wounded soldiers. The Royal Post Office was soon discontinued and Franklin installed the postal system that was the beginning of the present mail service in the United States. When the first postage stamps came into being, Ben's face appeared on the five-cent stamp.

Ben started mail delivery to people's houses by sending out mail not called for at the post office. For this service a small charge was collected. When letters remained unclaimed, he advertised them in the *Gazette,* and if they were still unclaimed after three months they were sent to a storeroom in Philadelphia. This was the beginning of the dead-letter office.

Franklin had delivered his own newspaper, the *Gazette,* by employing horseback riders, but he stopped this and sent his newspapers through the mail. What was most important, he made the postmasters and the couriers who actually carried the mail realize the importance of their work and the necessity of getting the mail through. The speed and safety of mail service made it very popular, for it drew distant parts of the thirteen colonies closer together. The postal service, made possible by Franklin, helped to cement the scattered colonies into one country.

Another thing that worried Franklin was the lack of military defense in Philadelphia, and he set out to enroll the citizens of Philadelphia. He realized the need when pirates from France and Spain invaded two plantations near Newcastle, Delaware, captured a ship coming from the West Indies, and murdered its captain.

At once Franklin got busy. He tried to persuade the Assembly to vote money for guns and defense, but the Quakers who controlled the legislature were peace-loving and had no quarrel with other nations. The rich merchants wouldn't give money since the Quakers wouldn't. Nobody seemed very interested in the matter, so Franklin took it to the people. *They* were interested.

At his first mass meeting in Robert's Coffee House, 1,200 persons signed up for a defense association. The association spread through the province until there were ten thousand members. They divided themselves up into companies and became a full-fledged militia. The women took up collections among themselves and made flags of silk for the various companies, embroidering or painting mottoes on them.

To arm his men, Franklin borrowed cannons from the Governor of New York. Though Ben had been elected a colonel of his militia, he refused the honor and served as a common soldier, manning cannons on the battery when his turn came.

It began to get around that every pie Ben Franklin had a finger in turned out well. So when a man named Thomas Bond needed help, he turned to Franklin.

Bond had been trying to get a hospital for the sick and insane built in Philadelphia, but he had failed because such institutions were unknown in America.

Ben immediately became interested in the hospital, for he was interested in everything. He wrote articles in the *Gazette* to get subscriptions and begged for money himself. Then he took up the matter with the Assembly. Finally he got a grant and a charter. He had the pleasure of writing the inscription for the cornerstone of the new hospital, which was opened in 1755, and he was elected president of the board.

This was the beginning of the great Pennsylvania Hospital of today. People who had never been cared for outside their homes, except in almshouses or jails, had a place to receive good care when they became ill.

When you hear how many things Ben Franklin did, you wonder how he ever found the time. The fact is, he never wasted time. Perhaps he lived by the rule he wrote down in *Poor Richard's Almanac:* "Early to bed and early to rise, makes a man healthy, wealthy and wise."

Anyway, that's the kind of man Ben turned out to be.

7

Inventor

Of all the men who were alive when America was young, Ben Franklin would be the most at home if he could come back here today. More than 170 years ago he wrote: "The rapid progress true science makes occasions my regretting sometimes that I was born so soon. It is impossible to imagine the height to which may be carried, in a thousand years, the power of men over matter."

Ben wouldn't be at all surprised to see washing machines washing clothes, penicillin curing people of their illnesses, families watching television programs, and spaceships landing on the moon.

You could not name anything that Benjamin Franklin wasn't interested in, and as has been seen, he was not only interested in what was going to happen in the future. He also thought about ways of improving the lives of the people who were living in his own time.

The very cold winter weather of Philadelphia was one subject to which he gave thought. Sometimes when he sat in front of his smoky fireplace, burning his face and knees while his back was left to freeze, it seemed to him that it was time to improve heating systems. He had noticed that heated air rises and cold air rushes in to take its place. Fireplaces of that day, with small openings, and more draughts than heat, did not take advantage of this fact. So he worked out the plan for an open stove that gave out more heat and used less fuel.

Franklin put this stove in his own house. He soon found that his family—especially the women, who were apt to stay at home and sit by the fire—got fewer colds and not so many toothaches.

One of his good friends, Robert Grace, had an iron foundry and Ben showed him a model of the stove.

"Why don't you go to work and make up some of these to sell to the people?" Ben said. "I've been using this contraption in my common room and it is twice as warm as it used to be for one-quarter the wood I used to burn there."

"I can make it, but how can I sell it?" Robert Grace asked. "I'm just an ironmonger."

"I'll put a piece in the *Gazette* about it," Ben said.

He sat down and wrote a long description of the stove. The article began by saying how much more comfortable the stove could make a room, and how the big fires people had to have in fireplaces to keep warm dried out their skins, dulled their eyes, and made them look *old*. With the Franklin stove, he went on, this didn't have to happen. (This made everyone in Philadelphia want a Franklin stove!)

In the rest of the article he explained the way the stove worked. To this he added a list of its advantages and answered in advance any objections that might come up. He then gave complete instructions for installing the stove in any fireplace.

As a further aid to Robert Grace, whose ironworks was in Chester County, not in Philadelphia proper, Franklin put in a stock of stoves at the post office, where he was postmaster.

Then he published his article in a pamphlet, instead of in the *Gazette,* and began to circulate it. The pamphlet excited plenty of interest and Governor Thomas, who was then head of the Colony of Pennsylvania, offered Ben a patent which would prevent anybody else from selling it.

Ben refused. He said: "As we enjoy great advantages from the invention of others, we should be glad of an opportunity to serve others by any invention of ours."

The Franklin stove was the first improvement in heating in many long years. People were delighted to have heat that made them more comfortable and was less expensive at the same time. Franklin stoves were soon in style, and shortly afterward they came into general use. (You can still see Franklin stoves today.) They undoubtedly improved the health of the colonists and influenced the design of stoves for years to come. They were much admired in Europe and copied in England. History notes that two were sent as presents to Leopold, Grand Duke of Tuscany.

Ben never lost his interest in better heating. He liked comfort and felt cold most of the time. He was always poking his nose up chimneys to see whether or not something couldn't be done to make them work better. He wrote a long letter on "The Cause and Cure of Smoky Chimneys" to one of his scientist friends after he became a very old man. During the winter of 1771, when he was living in London, he invented a new stove for burning coal. He used this stove in London and later at home in Philadelphia; and when he went to France as ambassador he took it along.

Benjamin Franklin's inventions were usually the result of observation—of looking at everything he saw and trying to figure out some better way of making things work. Many of his conclusions did not result in inventions of his own or anybody else's during his lifetime. He was too busy to do everything he thought of. But many of his thoughts were unheard of during the time in which he lived —a time full of superstition and general ignorance about the world of science as we know it.

One day he was taking a walk and he noticed a field where the grass was greener in some spots than in others.

I wonder why that is, Ben asked himself, and made it his business to find out.

He discovered that some letters had been traced on the field with gypsum, and where the gypsum had been dropped, the grass was greener.

"Gypsum should be spread on farms to improve the crops," Ben said. Most people thought he was crazy. They had never heard of artificial fertilizer. There wasn't any such thing, but now we know how important it is.

It was Ben, too, who said that farmers ought to be able to take out insurance on their crops against storms, blights, and insects. People were horrified that he should suggest such a thing. It was flying in the face of Providence! But such insurance is commonplace today.

He was a great one for walks, and that's where he got a lot of his ideas. He was following a stream one day when he saw an old woven basket lying in it. The reeds from which the basket was made had sprouted in the water and were putting out little green leaves.

"This basket is alive!" Ben said, and took home a couple of the sprouted sticks to raise. This wasn't exactly an invention, but it was the beginning of willow trees on the American continent.

Philadelphia was hot in the summer, and Ben's interest in his own comfort kept him busy experimenting. He decided, from watching reapers in a field, that evaporating perspiration kept the body cool. He experimented with this by having a steaming punch made of hot water, honey, and vinegar, and drinking it when the thermometer stood at a hundred. This induced perspiration and it made him feel cooler.

He also experimented with the effects of heat on dark cloth. He did this in the winter. He cut a few squares of black, dark blue, light blue, and white cloth and laid them on top of the snow in the direct rays of the sun. The black cloth had soon melted down into the snow. The dark blue was only slightly less buried. The light blue melted the snow slightly, but the white cloth lay on top of the snow at the end of the experiment. This convinced Ben that light color resisted heat and that light-colored clothing was more suitable for hot weather.

Ben was as interested in health as he was in comfort, and he had a good many interesting ideas on the subject. He noted that people who worked with certain metals—makers of printing type, plumbers, potters, and painters—were often sick of the same disease. It occurred to him that all these workmen handled white lead. He decided that lead was poison and that people who worked with it too long were poisoned by it. He was the first to diagnose lead poisoning, though he was not a medical doctor.

As he grew older and his eyesight failed, Ben found that he had to have two pairs of glasses. One pair he used for reading and other close work, and one pair he used when he was walking around. So he was constantly having to carry around two pairs of glasses. The glasses that he used for reading he also wore when he was eating. But, when he was wearing his reading glasses, he could not distinguish the faces of the people across the table. This was a great bore, so he took his glasses to the lens maker and had them cut in two. Half of each glass was put into the lower part of spectacle rims. When he looked down he could then see to eat. When he looked out he could see people's faces. That was the beginning of bifocal spectacles as we know them today.

Franklin had a lot of colds and he became interested in the causes of colds. "Traveling in severe winters," he said, "I have suffered cold sometimes to an extremity only short of freezing, but this did not make me catch cold. As for moisture, I have been in the river every evening two or three hours for a fortnight together, when one would suppose that I might imbibe enough of it to take cold if humidity could give it, but no such effect ever followed. I have long been satisfied from observation . . . that people often catch cold from one another when shut up together in close rooms and coaches."

Franklin went on to say that he believed people caught colds from unclean beds and old clothes and old books and decayed animal matter. Although he had never heard of a germ or a virus, Franklin discovered for himself about as much about the common cold as we know today.

When Franklin was putting up books on his library shelves, he often wished his arms were longer. Shortly thereafter he invented an instrument made of a stick with a wire grasp on the end. You may still find the grocer using this device to take down your box of Wheaties from a high shelf.

About the same time Ben thought up a chair whose seat turned over to make a ladder to climb on. If there's a stepladder chair in your kitchen, it may interest you to know that Ben Franklin was the inventor of its ancestor.

On his trips to and fro across the Atlantic, Franklin had time to notice things. It took many weeks to get to England and he had only the ship to explore. If his vessel was waylaid by fog, he did not complain of the wet but began to think about the value and importance of lighthouses and how he could get more of them built in America.

He had once read that Greek sailors in olden days poured oil on the sea to still the waves in a storm. Once when he was going to London, he noticed that one of the ships in the convoy left a smoother wake than the others. The captain said this was because the cook emptied grease out of the scullery in the ship's wake.

This information fascinated Franklin, who had a cane built containing a small bottle of oil. When walking beside a lake with his friends, he would use his cane to play a practical joke. First he would wager that he could make the waves stop.

People always took his bet. Then Ben would take his bamboo cane in hand and make a few magic passes over the water and wave the cane in the air three times. The waves would gradually sink and become smooth. This was because the oil he carried in the joint of his cane actually made them smooth.

On his trips across the Atlantic, he noticed a path of water that was of a different color from the rest of the sea. We know now that it was the Gulf Stream, that warms the shores of the eastern part of the United States. Franklin studied this phenomenon, before any other scientist ever heard of it. He provided a chart for sea captains that enabled them to take advantage of the current for swifter sailing. Thus, American ship captains were able to make faster time than English ship captains, because they sailed straight across the Gulf Stream instead of driving against the current for days.

Franklin always looked for the Gulf Stream when he crossed the ocean. He discovered that there were no whales in it. He noted that it was a different color from the rest of the ocean, and that more weeds grew in it. He found that it did not sparkle in the night. He learned that its water had a different temperature from the sea around it. All these facts led him to decide that it was really a river that ran through the ocean instead of through dry land. Nobody had ever noticed these things before.

Ben Franklin was on his way to France in 1776 when the colonies were already at war. He would have been hanged for treason if the *Reprisal* on which he sailed had been captured, but he did not bother to be frightened about this. He was too busy taking the temperature of the Gulf Stream!

Ben must have been a great comfort to the other inventors of his day, for such men are frequently thought to be a little crazy by the public, their families, and their friends. Ben did not believe that anything was impossible, and since he was known all over the world as a man of influence and power, his interest in the work of inventors was apt to give it public importance. When the first balloon went up in Paris, France, he was right on hand to witness the event.

The balloon, which was of silk and filled with gas made by pouring vitriol on iron filings, was the object of much laughter and joking. Some fifty thousand people had come out to scoff at it. As they laughed in the pouring rain, the balloon rose, went up until it seemed no larger than an orange, and disappeared in the clouds.

The crowd was surprised but they weren't willing to admit themselves wrong.

"It goes up," somebody said, "but what good is it?"

"What good is any newborn baby?" Ben demanded. "You will have to wait until it grows up!"

Franklin prophesied that ships that flew through the air might someday become a common means of travel, relieving the people of being jolted over the paving stones. Not in *his* time, of course, but someday! He also said that such flying ships might convince nations of the folly of war, since nobody could guard a country against air attack. He said the time might come when whole armies could be carried in balloons, and that it would cost much less to invade a country that way. Thus, as you can see, Franklin prophesied modern paratroopers. It is too bad that nations have not been able to convince themselves of the folly of war, as he predicted they might.

When he was not too busy with everything else, Franklin loved to listen to music. You will not be surprised to hear that he invented a musical instrument that was once very popular. It was actually a set of musical glasses, each of which he had blown in the shape of a hemisphere with a hole in the middle. The largest glass was nine inches across and the smallest three inches across.

Ben took thirty-seven of these glasses and tuned

them by grinding them, using a harpsichord to give him the true pitch. He mounted the glasses on an iron spindle, with the largest glasses at each end of the spindle and the smallest in the middle. The spindle was then placed horizontally in a case with four legs. The player, sitting before the spindle, revolved it with a pedal, such as was found on a spinning wheel in those times, and touched the edges of the moving glasses with his fingers.

Franklin said: "The advantages of this instrument are that the tones are incredibly sweet beyond those of any other; that they may be swelled or softened at pleasure by the stronger or weaker pressure of the fingers; that the instrument being once well-tuned never wants tuning."

Franklin called the instrument the armonica. Eventually it was called the harmonica. It was very popular in its day and great musicians gave concerts on it. Mozart and Beethoven both composed music for Franklin's instrument. Franklin played the harmonica, as well as the harp, guitar, and violin. He and his daughter, Sally, often amused themselves with duets, Sally playing the harpsichord and singing, and Ben playing the harmonica.

Ben Franklin first heard of electricity in 1746 while he was on a visit to Boston. There he met a Dr. Spence, who had just come from Scotland with some apparatus for making experiments. Franklin became so interested in the subject that he began to experiment with electricity himself when he got home. When Dr. Spence arrived in Philadelphia, Ben bought his equipment.

It is hard to imagine the excitement that surrounded this strange new thing in the world. Ben was so fascinated that he could think of nothing else. He spent most of his time with bits and pieces of household goods with which he made his first experiments—a salt cellar, a vinegar bottle, a pump handle, and gold from the binding of a book. He made little machines for himself to trap the electric spark, and demonstrated it to his friends. Soon his house was crowded with people who came to stare at the novelty, and he had no time for anything else.

A local glass blower copied Dr. Spence's equipment and before long several of Ben's friends were making experiments. This must have been a relief to Mrs. Franklin, since it took some of the load off her house.

Within a year, Franklin had made two of his most important discoveries—his conception of electricity as a single fluid, and his discovery of the positive and negative nature of currents. He also spoke often of the effect of pointed objects in attracting and throwing off electric fire. This was the beginning of his famous lightning rod.

Of course, he made many mistakes, and admitted them freely. His experiments were carried on not in a laboratory but in the common room of his home, and he had almost nothing to work with. With eleven panes of window glass, some thin lead plates, silk cord, and lead wire, Franklin produced the first electrical battery in history. He had absolutely no way of knowing how important this invention would become.

One of the things that worried Ben most about electricity was that he could not find any way to make it useful to people. He felt that it ought to benefit mankind in some way, instead of being a sort of freak sideshow for the curious. But if Ben Franklin had not continued with his experiments, we might not be using electricity now in all the hundreds of ways it serves us.

In those early years, electricity was almost a fad, like a new game. Nobody realized its powers, least of all Ben. He and his friends played with it, unaware of its dangers. They didn't bother with it much in the summer, for there were other things to do, so as hot weather came on they decided to end their experiments for the season with an electrical picnic.

They chose a spot on the banks of the Schuylkill River and set up their equipment. They proposed to kill a turkey by means of an electric spark, and roast it on an electric jack before a fire started in an electric bottle. Ben was conducting the show, and while he was going about killing the turkey with an electric spark, he failed to pay attention to what he was doing, for everybody was talking and laughing.

Suddenly there was a crack like a pistol shot, a terrific flash of fire, and Mr. Franklin took the entire charge through his body. Fortunately, although it was enough to kill the turkey, it wasn't enough to kill a man. Ben was knocked insensible, as if he had been struck from head to foot with one great blow. The hand that had held the chain conducting the charge turned white and numb, and he felt pretty numb all over most of the night. This was the nearest Ben ever came to being electrocuted.

Benjamin Franklin had twelve reasons for suspecting that lightning and electricity were the same thing. Both gave light. Both were the same color. Both took crooked directions. Both were swift in motion. Both were conducted by metals. Both made a noise in exploding. Both seem to exist in water or ice. Both tore bodies they passed through. Both destroyed animals, melted metals, set fire to inflammable material, and made a sulfurous smell.

Still, Franklin felt he had no proof that they were the same thing. Electricity was attracted by points. He decided to try to find out if lightning also was attracted by a sharp point. He wrote several articles about this and in many of them he outlined the need for sharp-pointed spires for buildings with ground wires. This belief eventually resulted in his invention of the lightning rod. But this line of thinking was more difficult to follow than the experiments he put on in his parlor, and people didn't pay much attention to it.

Ben felt it would be necessary to draw lightning from a cloud to prove that it was electricity, and he began to consider how this could be done. In some way he would have to get a sharp point up high in the air—perhaps on the top of a church steeple. Then he thought of a simpler method. He decided to fly a kite.

Nobody knows the hour or the day that this great historical event took place. Ben never mentioned it in any of his writings. It must have been one stormy afternoon in spring when Ben and his son William, who was twenty-one years old at the time (and not the small boy that most pictures show), started across the fields under the dark skies, holding the

85

kite out of harm's way and away from the eyes of the curious. They were both a little too old to fly kites and the experiment was conducted in the greatest secrecy. Ben was afraid people would poke fun at anything that looked so silly.

The kite was made of two crossed sticks of cedar over which a silk handkerchief had been tightly stretched and then tied at each point of the cross. It was fitted with a tail, a loop, and a ball of string. To the top of the upright stick of the cross, there was attached a sharp-pointed wire, which rose one foot above the crosspiece of wood. To the end of the string by which the kite was held, Ben tied a silk ribbon with a metal key.

Ben looked up at the threatening thunderclouds and handed the kite to William. "Run down the meadow, son," he said, "and let's get this contraption into the air."

William set off at a gallop and soon the silk kite was sailing toward the dark clouds. Although they flew it into several promising thunderheads, nothing happened. Ben was discouraged. He was on the point of hauling the kite down, rolling up the string, and going home for some dry clothes.

Suddenly he noticed that the fibers of the string he held in his hand were beginning to stand apart like hair on the back of a frightened dog.

"Look!" Ben shouted to William. "It's beginning to work."

At this moment he received the tingle of an electric shock from the key in the palm of his hand. Who can describe the emotions of a man at such a time? Ben may have felt triumph, exaltation, wonder, awe; but we have no way of knowing. Of all the things he ever did, this was probably the most far-reaching in its importance.

As the rain pelted down and the string became soaked, the electricity began to conduct freely through the key. Always practical, Ben Franklin produced a bottle he had brought along for the purpose, just in case, and began to trap the electricity in the glass bottle.

This was a great moment in the history of electricity. Ben, himself, must have been overcome with wonder, because he never said much about it. He talked about almost everything else. The reports of the discovery did not come out for several years.

As soon as his experiment was made known, Ben was given honorary degrees by Harvard, Yale, and William and Mary College. His fame spread rapidly, although the quick means of communication which have since been made possible by electricity, were not known in those days. Franklin had brought fire from the heavens with a homely toy, such as you yourself may have played with, and the world cheered.

He had also proved, as he had done many times before, that there is no end to what can be done with the simplest materials.

8

Statesman

A statesman is a man who is so wise and fearless that he is called on to help solve the problems of a whole country. It was natural that Ben Franklin became one of the great American statesmen. He had done so many good things for the people in Philadelphia that they wanted him to be a part of the government and to fight all their battles for them.

Ben had never thought much about taking part in the government. He had kept pretty busy being a good citizen, thinking up inventions, and working for a living. He wasn't very good at making speeches, and when he went to meetings, he sat quietly and listened and didn't say anything unless somebody asked him for his opinion. He was no orator. But as his business prospered and he began to have more leisure, he became the first person people thought about when it came to getting something done.

His public career started when the governor appointed him a justice of the peace. In this position it was his duty to sit on the bench and try cases. The corporation of Philadelphia made him a member of the city council and then an alderman. In 1751 he was elected a burgess of the Pennsylvania Assembly.

He already knew a good deal about the Pennsylvania Assembly and the laws it made. For fifteen years he had been the clerk who took all the laws down in handwriting. Being clerk of the Assembly had been a hard job and often dull, for the members argued and quarreled and wasted time the way people still do at meetings. When the debates dragged, Ben would sometimes entertain himself by making up one of his magic squares in arithmetic. Still, he had worked hard at his clerkship because it paid a salary. It had also helped him to get jobs printing ballots, laws, money, and stationery from the government.

When Ben became a member of the Assembly, elected by the people and representing them, he paid close attention to the debates. He also tried to get laws passed that would benefit everybody, but at first he was like a freshman at school. Nobody paid much attention to him. The laws he worked on were little laws about how many dogs should be allowed in the city limits of Philadelphia and where to put a bridge over the Schuylkill River. But pretty soon, the whole Assembly began to notice Ben and to realize that when he said something, it meant something.

In two short years he became a leader and they sent him off to Carlisle, Pennsylvania, to make a treaty with the Indians. Ben's handling of this matter was probably unconventional, but it resulted in a treaty. The Indians were very fond of rum and when they were drunk they were disorderly. As head of the commission to make the treaty, Franklin forbade that any liquor be sold to them.

The more than one hundred Indians who were living in temporary cabins around a hollow square outside Carlisle complained bitterly. Ben told them that as soon as the business was over, plenty of rum would be given them. When the Indians agreed, the treaty was conducted in good order and completed with unusual speed.

After the signing of the treaty, the rum was delivered. That night, when Ben and the members of his commission were sitting down to supper, they heard the most horrid yelling and savage cries coming from the Indians' encampment. They raced down there to see what on earth had happened.

The Indians had built a tremendous bonfire in the center of the square and were all wildly running around it, beating each other with firebrands, dancing, and making a fearful racket. The scene looked like a picture of hell, but Ben did not think anything could be done about it, so he and his friends returned to the inn and went to bed. In the middle of the night there was a pounding on the door. The Indians were there, howling for more rum, but Ben refused to get up.

The Assembly was very pleased with the treaty and seemed to think Ben had handled the situation masterfully. This was the beginning of his career in diplomacy. It was a wild and primitive beginning, but Ben lived in a wild and primitive country.

In 1754, when war with France was threatening, Franklin was once more sent to treat with the Indians. A congress of commissioners from all the colonies went to Albany to meet with the chiefs of the Six Indian Nations, and Ben was a member of the Pennsylvania delegation.

During his journey to Albany, Ben drew up the first plan for a union of the American colonies under one government for purposes of defense and the general good. This plan was rejected both by the colonial Assemblies and the English Crown, but it contained the germ of the United States.

One of Ben Franklin's qualities as a statesman was his ability to get along with everybody. During this period the representatives of the English king in Pennsylvania were in constant disagreement with the Assembly, where Franklin was a member of the colonial opposition. He never became personal in his political wrangles with the governor and various officials sent over from England. He was usually called on to carry the Assembly's complaints to the authorities.

The Assembly of Pennsylvania finally decided that the instructions they received from the governor and other officials worked too much of a hardship on the people of Pennsylvania. So the Assembly decided to take the matter up with the king. They appointed Ben their agent to go to London.

This was an important commission and made Ben feel a little nervous. He never expected to see the king. He knew it would take a long time to get his foot in the doorway of any important man in the English government. Nevertheless, he was prepared to do anything, for he felt the cause was right.

"You'll get yourself some fine clothes, now," said

Deborah, his wife. "And look out after yourself in that cold damp of London, won't you, Pa?"

"I'll take William with me," Ben said. "I'll put him to school and he'll keep me company."

"When will you be back?" she asked wistfully.

"Not long, not long," he said. "By the winter, mayhap."

It was March of the year 1757.

Ben and William set off in high spirits, but they ran into a long delay in New York and had a terrible trip. Storms and fogs followed the ship and so did the French pirates. Several times it seemed to Ben that he would never reach England. When he did arrive, he did just what American tourists do now. He made a sightseeing trip to Stonehenge, the great rocks in the South of England, and stopped off to see beautiful Salisbury Cathedral. He loved England and had many friends there.

Ben and William reached London on July 26, 1757. (They had left Philadelphia on April 4.) They took lodgings with a widow on Craven Street, Mrs. Margaret Stevenson, and William Franklin was entered in the Middle Temple to study law.

Father and son had four rooms and two servants and lived in luxury, as befitted an agent who was going to petition a king. Ben's account books show purchases of silver shoes and knee buckles, wigs, swords, cambric for shirts, handkerchiefs, and razors. He also shipped two cases of presents home to his wife, Deborah, and to his daughter, Sally. Among the gifts were crimson satin cloaks, muffs and stoles, English china, linen, dress goods, blankets, tablecloths, napkins, and a carpet for the "best room."

In a few months Ben hired a carriage, and before long he had settled down to life in London. He expected to go back to Philadelphia in a few months, but it was five years before he got home. During this time he pleaded the cause of the Pennsylvania Assembly wherever and whenever he got a chance. His problems were largely concerned with taxes, which the English Crown insisted on levying on the colonists, but not on the estates of their representatives. He also tried to smooth out the wrangles between the English governors and the members of the Assembly.

Sometimes a statesman achieves best results not by making speeches but by having persistence and winning small points, one at a time. This was Benjamin Franklin's method, and he made progress. He did so at the expense of his own leisure, and his devotion to duty kept him away from home and family for years on end.

The next time the Assembly sent him to Europe,

he stayed four years. By this time the American colonists were really upset about the taxes England kept heaping on them. Franklin tried to pour oil on the troubled waters, the way he used to pour oil from his cane onto the little waves of a ruffled lake. Daily he made his rounds of all the great men he could reach in England, trying to get something done about America.

It wasn't easy to leave his home, his family, and his friends, and stay all those years in another country, fighting to protect the rights of the colonies and still keep the peace. Nor was his cause popular. In both England and America he had many enemies. When the Stamp Act was passed in England, he saw the careful plans of years swept away; and in America, his enemies threatened to set fire to his house. He felt that he was a failure. His mail to his son in America was tampered with, and the letters he received from home had been opened. He had spells of terrible homesickness and spoke often of giving up and coming home. Still he fought on, counseling patience at home, urging his contacts in England to consider what might happen if the colonists were made too angry.

When the Boston Tea Party took place, fuel was added to the fire. Ben was in London and he wanted to be in America. "I suppose," he wrote, "that never since we were a people have we had so few friends in Britain."

But like a true statesman, Franklin stayed on and fought on. He was getting old and he was troubled with gout, colds, and other ailments. He was lonely and homesick, but he still hoped against hope that the few friends of America in England might persuade the government to see the light.

Then his wife, Deborah, died in Philadelphia and Franklin started his sad journey home on the next boat. He knew that war was coming and he was afraid it would be a long war. For more than ten years he had fought against that war, believing that peace would be best for both England and the colonies. He had failed in his mission. He shed tears over the unhappy future but he knew that his heart lay forever with America.

9

Patriot

Ben Franklin had lived three score and ten years before the shot that was heard around the world was fired at Lexington. Old men of seventy are not often in favor of revolutions, but Franklin was an unusual man. He did not feel old. He had spent years trying to avoid this war, but as soon as it was clear that nothing could be done to avoid it, he took his stand for America. He was the oldest member of the Continental Congress, but he was made a deputy in the Congress as soon as he got to Philadelphia.

Franklin did almost everything in the American Revolution except carry a gun. If necessary, he would have done that. He was immediately placed on the Committee of Safety, which never stopped work throughout the whole war. He was on the Committee in Charge of Indian Affairs. He organized the militia. He was put in charge of Home Defense. He was on the Committee for Foreign Affairs, and on a Committee to Correspond with Friends Abroad. This was the beginning of the State Department.

He raised money and lent and gave his own to the cause of the colonists. He got medicine, food, and guns for the American troops. He wrote letters, reports, and resolutions, and helped with all the important documents of a new nation. He continued, at the age of seventy, to make hazardous journeys.

The first report brought in by Franklin's Committee for Foreign Affairs—and one that appeared in his own handwriting—was the news that the people in Canada were not in sympathy with the American cause. They needed to have it explained to them. Franklin learned of this on February 14, 1776, and in March set out for Canada with a party of younger men.

In Saratoga, where the snow was six inches

deep, they stayed a week, waiting for the ice to melt on Lake George so a boat could get through. Ben, who had begun to feel old in the middle of desperately cold weather and hard living, did not expect to live through this trip. He sat down and wrote letters of farewell to several of his friends.

At last the ice began to break up in the lake and they started across on clumsy flatboats that were without heat or even roofs. The weather was wet and raw and every now and then the men had to land on the shore, get off the boats, cut wood, and start a fire to keep themselves from freezing. Most of the party slept in the woods at night, but Ben, because of his advanced age, slept under an awning on the open boat.

When they reached the other side of Lake George, they got off and went on foot to the shores of Lake Champlain. Here they took to boats again. They would start before daybreak, pull in to shore to make fires when they were freezing, and then push on once more. They finally arrived at St. John's, where they hired carriages to take them to the St. Lawrence River and another boat. They arrived in Montreal about a month after they had left Philadelphia, and were received by General Arnold.

Franklin had all but given his life to this mission, but he realized from the moment he entered into conference with General Arnold that it would not succeed. The American colonies had neither money nor credit. Franklin had paid for most of this trip out of his own pocket. British reinforcements were pouring into Quebec. Franklin was sick with a siege of boils. He decided to go home. He and his party made their painful way back to Philadelphia and the old man went to bed for several weeks.

As the boils subsided, Franklin's spirits rose and he was soon again in the thick of the Continental Congress' affairs.

Ben, who was now called Dr. Franklin, with reverence and respect, was the most famous American in the world. He was as well known in Europe as in America, as well known in the world of science as the world of politics, as well known in literary circles as in diplomatic circles. He was a celebrity. When two servants in livery bore his sedan chair to the door of the State House where the Continental Congress sat for meetings, people crowded around just to look at him.

The sedan chair was the taxi of colonial Philadelphia. It was a chair, with a hood or cover, placed on two poles which were borne on the shoulders of strong servants. Ben, who loved walking better than anything, was reduced to a sedan chair by gout.

One young man, Philip Mackenzie of Charleston,

who was visiting in Philadelphia in the summer of 1776, describes Benjamin Franklin in a letter to a friend:

> He is about five feet nine. . . . He is too heavy for his height. His eyes are gray and they are keen and sharp as steel. His head is quite large. His forehead is high and he has a mole on the left cheek. No wig. He wears his hair long. It reaches to his shoulders. Strange to say, it is not yet white but only a little gray though he is seventy at least. Maybe I am wrong, but it seems to me that he is secretly amused and keeping it to himself. That is the sort of look in his eyes. Though he has conversed with most of the great people of the world, he listened intently to my silly remarks as if they were really interesting. After he left I said as much to Ed Rutledge and he laughed. "Don't fool yourself," he said, "Dr. Franklin was interested. You don't know him. He is interested in everything and everybody . . . who you are and what you have done all your life."

103

The very fact that Benjamin Franklin espoused the cause of the American Revolution made the world pay more attention to it. There were, of course, many people who lived in the colonies who did not take any stock in the Revolution and remained loyal to England. Franklin had strong ties in England and he had opposed war on principle, but when it came to the cause of freedom, he didn't even have to think about it. He had always been on that side.

Philadelphia was an exciting place in the days just before the war started. It was still the largest town in the American colonies, with a population of 40,000. Benjamin Franklin's determined efforts at civic improvement had made it one of the best. It had street lights, paved streets, brick footpaths to walk on, and a volunteer fire department.

Most of the shops and houses were painted; the people dressed well and ate well and loved both. They had four meals a day, beginning with coffee and rolls at seven, breakfast or lunch at eleven, dinner at four and supper about ten. The delegates to the Continental Congress, who came from all over the colony, gave people a new reason for having parties.

The people wore showy clothes—silver buttons, scarlet vests trimmed with gold lace, cocked hats, lace cuffs weighted with lead to make them hang down. They carried gold snuff boxes and wore swords, knee breeches, and silk stockings. The women wore hoop skirts so wide they had to walk sideways through a door, and fancy bonnets. At dinner parties there would often be fourteen courses; as a result a good many people developed the gout.

Franklin did not, in spite of his fame, go in for this kind of ostentation. He had a pleasant and comfortable house where he was always surrounded by friends and the most interesting people who came to Philadelphia. He enjoyed his home after his many years abroad, and he enjoyed the company of the representatives to the Continental Congress.

If you remember the signers of the Declaration of Independence, you will recall how many exciting minds were at work in Philadelphia that year. Franklin was the elder statesman of the Congress and one of the boldest, but he didn't say much.

"I never heard him speak more than ten minutes at a time, nor but to any but the main point to decide the question," Thomas Jefferson said.

But Ben kept everybody cheered up with his funny stories. He had a twinkling kind of humor and loved to make jokes.

While the wording of the Declaration of Independence was being fought over in the Congress, he sat by its author, Thomas Jefferson. Jefferson was unhappy because it seemed that each member of the Congress wanted to change something in the Declaration. He sat there with his handsome head in his hands, listening to them tearing his writing apart.

"It reminds me of John Thompson," Franklin said.

"Who was John Thompson?" Jefferson wanted to know.

Ben said John Thompson was a friend of his who had been apprenticed to a man who made hats. Finally he served out his time and opened his own shop. He wanted a signboard to let people know he made hats, so he drew a picture of a hat and wrote his advertisement, as follows: "John Thompson, hatter, makes and sells hats for ready money." He then started asking his friends what they thought of it. The first friend told him that he didn't need to say he was a hatter since he was also saying that he made and sold hats. Thompson took out the word "hatter." The next friend said that people wouldn't care much who made the hats so long as they could buy them, so why not take out the word "makes." Thompson obliged. The third friend said that it was silly to say "for ready money," since Thompson did not offer credit. Thompson left out "for ready money." All he had left now was: "John Thompson sells hats." His next friend pointed out that nobody would expect him to give hats away so why say "Sells hats?" Thompson admitted this was true. The sign then read: "John Thompson, Hats." Since a hat was already painted on the sign, there didn't seem to be much point in the word "Hats" so Thompson removed that. The sign ended up by being a picture of a hat with John Thompson's name under it.

Franklin said that was what happened to people's fine language when they asked somebody else about it. Jefferson laughed, as did everybody else who heard the story, and it may have dissuaded the Congress from cutting out more of Jefferson's beautiful writing in the Declaration of Independence.

The Declaration of Independence was at last made satisfactory to the Congress. When it was ratified, the greatest Americans of that time stood around, grave and worried, brooding over the things that could happen as a result of this courageous plunge into the future.

Can you imagine that scene in Independence Hall—the hot July day, the tense mood of the men gathered there (they had been voting on the Declaration for two or three days and nights), the blankness of the future? How much they stood to lose— their lands, their work, the safety of their wives and children, their very lives! They had little money, almost no military equipment, only the beginnings of an army. Yet they proposed to pit these things against the established superiority of the great English nation. Every man who stood waiting to add his name to the document must have been trembling inside.

Ben Franklin must have shared this general apprehension. He had expected to live out his days under the shelter of the English Crown. One of his early jobs as an agent had been an attempt to persuade the English to make Pennsylvania a Royal Province. He had worked hard from childhood for the security that money could bring and he was old enough to want to live in peace and rest. But he was a lover of liberty—a patriot. And he had the courage and spirit to fight for it.

Ben sized up the situation, and as America trembled on the brink of being born, he made everybody feel better by giving them a chance to laugh. He made a remark, which we would call a wisecrack these days. It lightened the eighteenth-century air, and made everybody feel brave, the way a wisecrack sometimes can.

In that still room in Philadelphia's Independence Hall, as the signers hesitated before putting their names to the revolutionary document, Franklin smiled and said: "We must all hang together, or assuredly, we shall all hang separately!"

After that he wrote his name.

10

Ambassador

The story of plain old Benjamin Franklin in Paris always reads a little like a fairy tale. No American, with the exception of Charles Lindbergh, a century and a half later, ever received such an exciting and tumultuous welcome in Paris as seventy-year-old Ben. The occasion was his arrival in France as Commissioner of the American Colonies, in December 1776. Strange to say, he was more popular in France than he was in America.

For some time the members of the Continental Congress in Philadelphia had been trying to select a man who would go to Europe to get help for the colonies in the war against England. They thought of everybody else before they got around to thinking about Benjamin. Thomas Jefferson was the first choice, but he refused to go because his wife was desperately sick. John Adams was mentioned, and he was very anxious to go, but the members felt he was too young. When Ben's name finally came up, there were enough people in the Continental Congress who were jealous of Franklin's popularity and reputation to look down their noses at the suggestion.

"Why, he isn't even a college graduate!" said some, and of course this was true. Ben had never been near a college except to accept some of the highest honorary degrees they could bestow. He had educated himself.

"I remember him when he didn't have a penny in his pocket," said others. This was true too; Ben had earned his own fortune.

"He can speak French, though," said John Witherspoon, the youngest member of Congress, who was fond of Franklin. "What good would a college graduate be able to do if he couldn't speak the language?" This was quite true, too. Ben had taught himself French; he wrote it fluently and spoke it ungrammatically.

"Well, if you want this servant to go," Ben said, after the Congress had finally voted him one of three members of a committee to go to France, "he will go!"

Ben's life was not particularly easy at this time. He missed his wife, Deborah, who had died three years before. He missed his many English friends, from whom he had been cut off by the war. He had lived in England for a long time and he had formed strong affections there. Many of the friends he had known and loved best in America were dead.

There were other things that brought him sorrow. His home and property were at times in the hands of the enemy. His only son had deserted the American cause to become a Tory. This was a matter of great grief to Franklin. The rising generation of Americans seemed to be jealous of his reputation and popularity. Ben had lived a hard life and his health wasn't good. He had gout and gallstones. He was seventy years old and it was time to think of resting, but he worked on, against all these odds.

When Ben got ready to go to France, he knew he might be there a long time. He didn't really know whether he would ever see his home again, and he didn't want to go alone. He decided to take his two

113

grandsons with him. They were both young. William Temple Franklin, the son of his only son, was sixteen, and Benjamin Franklin Bache, the son of his daughter, Sarah, was just a child.

The colonies were already in a shooting war with England, and crossing the Atlantic, which was never very simple in those days, was really frightening. In addition to wind and weather, the traveler had to think about the well-armed British Navy, which has always been efficient.

Ben and his two grandsons set sail on the *Reprisal* on October 26, 1776. The French knew that Franklin was coming, and the English knew it, too. The British spies had seen to that. If the English Navy could have captured the *Reprisal*, it would have been a great prize with Ben Franklin aboard. He would have been hanged as a traitor if he had been caught.

Winter on the Atlantic then, as now, was full of wind and storms, and all in all, it was a dangerous voyage. First a bad storm came up. Ben had to stay in his cabin with the portholes closed and couldn't take his exercise. He passed the time giving French lessons to his grandchildren. When he could get out on the deck he studied the Gulf Stream, but this wasn't often. Captain Wilkes, the captain of the *Reprisal*, was busy dodging English

114

cruisers and having a few fights on the way, and he didn't like to have his famous passenger in plain view.

Thirty-three days passed before the coast of France loomed ahead of them. Just off Brittany, the *Reprisal* got into a fight with two English merchant ships and captured them, so when she sailed into the Bay of Quiberon she escorted captives. But Ben was weak from confinement in his cabin and scarcely able to walk when he and the others went ashore.

"I must get on to Paris," Ben said. "I have work to do. Go hire a coach, William."

"It's a long way, Dr. Franklin," Captain Wilkes told him.

"The forests are full of robbers," said William. "That's what I heard!"

"Silver and gold have I none," Ben said. "Mayhap we can turn the tables and rob *them!*"

"Bandits have a habit of murdering poverty-stricken travelers," said Captain Wilkes.

"Alas," said Ben, "I still expect the gout to carry me off. Go look into the matter of a carriage."

When the carriage arrived, Ben wondered if it would hold together until they got to Paris.

"It suits me well," he said. "It is as old and infirm as I am, and probably of an age with me."

Into the broken-down old coach they piled—Ben and his two grandchildren, and all the trunks and bags and bundles and boxes that go with such a tour. Little Benjamin Bache considered it a great lark. William was not too pleased at the sorry old carriage and Ben, bouncing over the holes and ruts of the terrible road, through the dark woods, up hill and down dale, suffered all day. At night he would not let himself sleep. If there were murderers and bandits in the forests, he must be awake. He had responsibilities—the two young people depending on him there and the colonists depending on him in America.

As they made their painful way toward Paris, a strange thing happened. The French people began to line the roads to watch the carriage pass. They came out of their fields and shops and houses to watch the clattering coach with the old man in the Quaker-like brown coat inside and to raise a cheer.

Ben couldn't have been more amazed. He had been in France twice before and he loved the country and its people. Yet he did not suppose, in his modesty, that they had ever heard of him.

Almost everybody in the civilized world had heard of Dr. Franklin, and the revolt of the American colonies had excited and thrilled the French people. They were already brooding over a revolution of their own. Here was a man who came from a great wild continent, full of red Indians. He was representing a handful of people who had enough courage to fly in the face of rich, powerful England — to take up arms against authority and make a new world for themselves. The French were overcome with admiration.

As the carriage lumbered on, the news ran ahead of it. At Nantes, the city fathers put on a ceremony.

"Dr. Franklin!" they hailed. "Tonight we make a great banquet for you, and after that the ball!"

"That is most kind of you," Franklin said courteously, hanging on to his walking stick, for he was too tired to stand up. "Pray do not trouble yourselves unduly. I must push on to Paris with all speed."

"Only for tonight!" they chorused, and it was done.

Ben was too sick to eat and too weak to dance, but he charmed everybody who came within the sound of his voice. He could charm a bird off a tree.

When the coach left Nantes, the welcome gathered momentum like a snowball rolling downhill, or a tumbling tumbleweed. Flags were hung out in every town on the route. Everybody anywhere near the road swarmed to the roadside to pelt Ben with flowers. "Dr. Franklin! Dr. Franklin!" the people roared as he went by, and held up their babies to see him and ran out and touched the sleeve of his old brown coat.

Ben was more and more astonished to have such a fuss made over him. In England he had narrowly escaped being tried for treason. In America his enemies had tried to set fire to his house. But in France he was a hero. Well, you never knew what would happen next!

He wasn't what you would call handsome. As the representative of a raw, poor, backwoods country, he was plainly dressed. On his trip over he had got in the habit of wearing an old fur hat to protect his bald head from the sea breezes. It was a little too large and fell down over his broad forehead almost to his glasses.

That was another thing. He wore his spectacles all the time, because he couldn't see well without them and he couldn't bear to miss anything. Wearing spectacles in public was a novelty in the eighteenth century. People would stumble around half-blind before they would be caught wearing their glasses out of doors.

From under his fur hat, Ben's thin, gray, unpowdered, straight hair peeked out. He carried a plain walking stick instead of the sword usually worn

118

by gentlemen, and the French newspapers made a great point of his being unarmed. In that age of powdered and perfumed dandies, with their satin knee breeches, embroidered coats, and lace ruffles, Ben was a real curiosity.

When the journey came to its end and the coach wound its way down the narrow, crooked streets of old Paris, the welcome reached its full flower. Every shop window displayed pictures of Dr. Franklin, and Ben's plain, good-humored face was soon looking down over every mantelpiece in town. Rich and poor, famous and infamous, old and young, the population of Paris took Ben to its enthusiastic heart.

He moved into a hotel, but every time he appeared on the street, he stopped traffic. The people crowded around him, plucking at his coat sleeve, calling his name, and asking him questions. They stood outside the hotel, waiting for him to come out, and it soon became clear that he would never get any work done as long as this went on.

One of his friends, a rich Frenchman named Le Ray de Chaumont, invited Franklin and his grandchildren to come to his estate at Passy, a small village outside Paris. The American visitors could live in a little house in the garden of de Chaumont's estate.

So, bag and baggage, Ben moved to Passy and

there he stayed. His disappearance from the boulevards of Paris made him a man of mystery and increased the excitement about him. Soon people would travel up to Passy and throw notes and letters to Franklin over the garden wall.

These letters were addressed to "Monsieur Franklin in the Garden." They came from soldiers, adventurers, merchants, young hotheads who wanted to fight for liberty, French schoolboys, and ladies who just craved to make his acquaintance. Not satisfied with writing letters, they began to climb over the garden wall and storm the house. Franklin, who was interested in everybody, usually saw everybody who wanted to see him, and this made him get behind with his work.

It is hard to say what it was about Ben that made him so popular. He was fairly homely. Though he was famed as a scientist, there were many who had had better opportunities to study and become scholars, and who therefore knew more about science. At this time, he wrote more than he read, so he did not talk very easily about the books of the day. But he was honest and when he talked he never made flat statements. He would say: "I think it is like this," or "I imagine this is the way it is." And he knew people better than he knew books. Everybody learned to listen for his soft, low voice.

Many French people who got to know Ben wanted France to side openly with the American colonies and fight England. The French Government, however, could not afford an all-out war.

In Paris Ben worked for the colonies with Silas Deanne and Arthur Lee. After they arrived in the French capital, the three men were received in an audience by Charles Gravier, Count of Vergennes, who was the Foreign Minister of France. Vergennes told them that France must remain neutral. He told Ben, on the side, that he sympathized with his cause and would help where he could.

"Monsieur, le comte," Ben said one day, "there are several cannons being removed from the royal arsenal and loaded onto ships."

"Indeed," said Vergennes. "Where are these ships bound?"

"Nobody seems to know," said Ben.

"Good," said Vergennes. "I have not heard anything about this."

"I have not said anything," said Ben.

"If these ships should happen to pass under my window," said Vergennes, "I shall be looking in another direction."

In such a manner, Ben Franklin obtained guns, ammunition, and food for Washington's army. Without these supplies it might not have survived.

Franklin's friendship with Vergennes took him often to Versailles, the beautiful palace where the king and queen lived, and it was there he was presented to Louis XVI and Marie Antoinette.

When Ben appeared before the king for the first time, he was accompanied by twenty of his countrymen, two or three of whom wore uniforms. Franklin had a suit of reddish brown velvet, white silk stockings, and a white hat under his arm. His long gray hair hung loose on his shoulders and he was wearing his spectacles.

There is no record of what Ben said to the king, but the reply of the king was gracious, toward both Benjamin and his country. The king praised Ben's conduct.

From that time on, Ben went to the Court every Tuesday, along with diplomats of all other countries, though his title was in doubt. The French called him ambassador, but Americans called him a commissioner.

He had many meetings with King Louis and they became friends. Franklin always referred to the king, with affection, as "the young man." The king was in his twenties, a great, overgrown, fat boy, who loved to tinker with machinery—locks and clocks—and found a kindred spirit in the American scientist.

Through his close friendship with the French Court and Government, Ben obtained a loan for the American colonies of forty-five million French livres. In addition to this, he received from Louis a gift of ten million livres outright.

"If you are questioned regarding our opinion of Dr. Franklin," Vergennes said, speaking for the King of France, "you may say without hesitation that we esteem him as much on account of his patriotism as the wisdom of his conduct, and it has been owing in great part to this cause, and to the confidence we put in the veracity of Dr. Franklin, that we have determined to relieve the pecuniary embarrassment in which he has been placed by Congress."

Translated into ordinary talk, this meant that if Ben hadn't been there, France would never have let America have the money.

In addition to this, many people who had nothing to do with the French Government wanted to lend Franklin money for his cause.

One of his best friends, a very wealthy woman named Madame Helvetius, said: "I am going to offer my fortune to that good Franklin."

Ben carried on all his work with almost no help. It is easy to understand why he was unpopular with his helpers from America. Ben was a hero, but nobody had ever heard of the helpers and nobody mentioned their names. This made them feel unimportant—something that proud people do not like.

William, Ben's grandson, who was still a boy, served as his secretary, but Benjamin Bache was too young to do anything but go to school.

Few persons ever received more letters than Franklin and he felt as if he had to answer all of them.

He began to be asked to all kinds of parties and entertainments and he thought that he ought to attend them. He never knew when he would meet somebody who would be willing to help America.

All the great artists of France wanted to paint Ben's portrait, and he sat for many of them. His image was cast in more different forms than he would ever have thought possible. His face appeared on ladies' brooches and bracelets, on medallions worn around the neck, on the tops of boxes and the sides of vases, on plaques to hang on the wall, in portraits, and in sculptured busts.

"Don't you get tired of seeing yourself so often?" Sally Bache, his daughter, asked him once. "Everywhere I look I see you, Papa."

"There's one thing about it," Ben said. "It makes me good."

"It makes you vain," his daughter said teasingly.

"It makes me moral," Ben said. "I simply can't afford to do anything wrong."

"Why?"

"Because," her father told her, "I couldn't run away. My face is so familiar—such as it is—the police would catch me the first hour!"

All the great men of France wanted to meet him. Voltaire, the French philosopher, invited him to his home. Franklin went and took William. When they came into the room where the ailing old man was enthroned in a great chair, Voltaire leaned toward them. Then he said in English, "O Liberty, thou Goddess heavenly bright."

"This is my grandson, William Franklin," Ben said humbly. "Will you give him your benediction?"

"God and Liberty," said Voltaire, "this is the only benediction that is fit for a grandson of Mr. Franklin."

In writing about this, Voltaire said that "all those who were present shed tears of tenderness."

There is a story that Ben asked Voltaire if he could not bring little Benjamin Bache some weekend when he was home from school.

"I have another grandson," Ben said. "Would you give *him* your blessing?"

"But, of course," Voltaire replied.

125

When Ben brought his namesake, Voltaire lifted the child up and kissed him.

"Liberty and Equality!" he said. This was believed to be the beginning of the rallying cry of the French Revolution: "Liberty, Equality, and Fraternity." But who knows? It is just a story.

Franklin did not have either the money or the room to give parties and pay people back for the kindnesses they had shown him. Yet he was a hospitable soul, and as much as he could, he did have company. The parties were not much like those usually given by ambassadors. They were more like the parties held in American homes today, at which people sit around and talk.

As a matter of fact, it seems likely that Franklin invented the buffet supper. His little house in Passy was too tiny for a large number of diners, so in the soft months of French spring and summer, he would have trestles or sawhorses set up in the garden. Across them, boards would be laid and covered with a tablecloth. On these tables the food was placed.

Then, with a lack of ceremony unknown in diplomatic circles, the guests helped themselves and stood or sat around the flower gardens, eating. This was considered a quaint American custom by the French, and word of it appears in several letters of the times.

Franklin did have one formal party. On the Fourth of July, 1778, he celebrated the second birthday of American independence with a dinner for fifty gentlemen. John Adams, who had been sent to Paris to work with Franklin, was co-host for this, and that is why it was a more formal affair. John Adams was a formal man and disapproved of everything Ben did. If he gave a party, it would have to be correct.

The table for this birthday party was covered with flowers, and the American flag and the French Cap of Liberty were part of the centerpiece. From a big basket of flowers on the table, each guest received "a posy" with an inscription tied to it. After dinner, thirteen toasts were drunk, one to each of the thirteen original colonies.

11

Friend

Of all the things that Benjamin Franklin did, perhaps the most important was to make friends. His love of people never failed him once during his long life, and his friends played a large part in his life.

Although he was a doer of great deeds, Franklin was first, last, and always a human being who loved pleasure and entertainment and company. He liked to play checkers and chess and cribbage almost as much as he loved to read, and he liked to talk. He enjoyed clubs and was always gathering groups of friends into organizations where they could exchange ideas and friendship. "I like to converse at large with such ingenious and worthy men as are pleased to honor me with their friendship," he said.

The first of the groups that Ben organized was the Leathernapron Club in Philadelphia, which he started when he was a young man. Later known as the Junto, it had a far-reaching effect on Ben's life. The members of the Junto were his first tried-and-true friends, and they remained so for as long as they and he lived. It was in this little circle that he learned to be a leader of men. There he discovered that people who trust each other and work together can accomplish much more than one man working alone. With the help of these friends, Franklin became an important person much earlier than he would have become otherwise, although this had not been the purpose of forming the club. He had started it because he liked to be with people he loved.

Many of the great events of his life, and many of those that most affected this country, were brought about by Franklin's friendships. His ability to win people to himself furthered the cause of American liberty.

From the very beginning, his friends could not do enough for him. John Collins helped him to escape from his hated apprenticeship. Ben went into business with Hugh Meredith, who so enjoyed

Franklin's friendship that he persuaded his father to lend them the money to open a print shop. His first customers were brought to the shop by his friends, who helped his business to prosper.

Most of the great honors that were awarded Ben were arranged by friends who held him dear. He had more real friends than anybody else alive when he was on earth, and his fame continues to be brightened by the friends he has made with his books and writings.

Franklin loved all his friends, but he was especially fond of boys and girls. He made friends of his own children and all the other children who came into his life. He was a champion of youth and always made young people happy by not considering them a different kettle of fish but exactly the same as grown people. He listened to what they had to say with the same interest he gave to governors and prime ministers. He paid attention to what they said and he learned from them, so that although he lived to be over eighty, he never grew old in his mind and heart.

When Franklin was forced by his duties to live away from home in England and France, he always was surrounded by children, because he was not happy without them. In England he often visited in the home of Jonathan Shipley, a bishop,

who had one son and five daughters. The girls
ranged in age from twenty-three to eleven, and
they adored Benjamin Franklin. He once took Kitty
Shipley, age eleven, on a trip to London. As a present to the Shipley girls, he sent to Philadelphia
for a gray squirrel which became the great pet of
the household. The squirrel, who was called Skugg,
was finally killed by a dog, and at the request of
the girls Franklin wrote for it his famous epitaph:

> Here Skugg
> Lies snug
> As a bug
> In a rug.

When Franklin lived at Passy as Ambassador to
the Court of France, he had Benjamin Bache on
his knee a good part of the time. He said in one of
his letters that although he was busy and often
tired, he invited little Benjamin's friends to supper
one day a week. He was popular with all the children of his French friends in Passy, and most of
them called him Papa.

French schoolboys wrote him long letters, and
he answered them. When John Jay, one of Franklin's friends, lived for a few months at his house,
Jay's 1½-year-old daughter, Maria, formed a great

132

affection for Franklin. She followed him around like a little puppy.

After Franklin's young friends grew up and married and reared families of their own, he petted and teased and played with the new generation. He thought nothing of inviting three or four children to spend a summer or a year or even several years in his house, and it always rang with the shouts of his young friends.

Some of Ben Franklin's most wonderful letters were written to children, and he was forever thinking up little presents and treats to please them. In his will Franklin left a sum of money (one hundred pounds) to the free schools of Boston. The interest on this money was to be used for the purchase of silver medals to be presented as honorary awards to boys. These medals are still given out in the Boston Latin School and in the high schools of Boston. So his friendship for children lives after him.

In France, Franklin's friends numbered about the same as the population of the country, including everybody from the king and queen to the humblest workman.

"I could never forget the nine years of happiness I enjoyed in the sweet society of these people," Franklin said.

He was seventy-nine when the Congress of the United States finally accepted his resignation and gave him permission to come home. This was in the year 1785. In 1783 he had negotiated the peace treaty between England and France and had seen it signed in Paris. He felt that his work was completed, and that younger Americans should take over. His friends in France could scarcely bear to see him go. He started his rounds to say good-bye.

When Louis XVI bade him farewell, he presented Ben with a medallion containing a small painting of the king surrounded by four hundred diamonds.

"If you must go," said Louis, "I will give you safe conduct to the coast. The royal mules will draw your litter."

This was a great honor!

When Ben set out for home, the litter and the royal mules led a procession of carriages, in which dozens of his friends rode to the great North Gate of Paris. When the gate was reached, his hosts in France for nine years, Monsieur de Chaumont and his daughter, could not turn back. They followed Franklin all the way to the sea.

Progress was slow, for in every village and town, welcoming committees came out and halted the mules. There were tears, speeches, great bouquets of roses, and little presents pressed in his hand by the children. Franklin, who was old and sick and full of aches and pains, bore up manfully. The slow motion of the litter kept him in agony, but he smiled and listened, climbed down from his perch, and shook the hands offered to him.

One distinguished Frenchman instructed his servants to detain Ben and keep him overnight at his chateau to give him much-needed rest. At last he came to the Channel and set sail for England, where he stayed a few days and then once more started across the Atlantic.

The last years of his life were peaceful. He was reconciled with his son, whose desertion of the American cause had wounded him deeply, and he was at last honored at home as he had been abroad. He was elected president of the Commonwealth of Pennsylvania, and later re-elected three times. He was appointed a delegate to the convention that framed the Constitution of the United States and played an important part in the making of this document which we still live by.

During these years, he lived with his daughter, Sally Bache, and her husband and family. Best of all, his friends, new and old, gathered around and kept him company. One of his last enthusiasms on earth was the abolition of slavery. In this, he was many years ahead of his time, for slavery was still common nearly a century later.

Ben kept going about his business, although he was so old; and this determination to be active, in spite of the gout, resulted in a fall on some stairs from which he was slow to get well. On April 17, 1790, he died, after a short illness, and the whole civilized world went into mourning. Drums were muffled, flags were dipped to half-mast, and funeral guns boomed wherever men stood together. The French Assembly, at the motion of his old friend Mirabeau, seconded by the Marquis de Lafayette, declared a three-day period of mourning. This was almost unheard of.

All the great personages of Philadelphia walked behind Franklin's coffin, followed by twenty thousand mourners, the largest crowd ever assembled in Philadelphia up to that time. Orations were written by all the great writers alive and spoken in public places by all the great orators. Humble men stood around on street corners and in the taverns and spoke their own little eulogies. Women wept openly in the streets, and children felt suddenly lost and lonely. A friend of man had gone out of the world.

12
American

It would take a bigger book than this one to tell all the things that Ben did for his country. If he had not lived, the United States of America might not hold the important position it now has in the world. His whole life is a record of achievements and most of them were directed toward improving his own country.

Here are some of the things Benjamin Franklin did:

He advocated paper money in America and helped encourage business.

He founded the first circulating library in America.

He organized the first volunteer fire department in Philadelphia.

He was one of the founders of the first hospital in Pennsylvania.

He became postmaster and reorganized the postal system so that it became efficient and profitable.

He founded the American Philosophical Society, which is still in existence.

He advocated the first paved streets and installed a street-cleaning system.

He modernized the street-lighting system.

He advocated home defense and founded the Pennsylvania militia.

It was Franklin who first conceived a union of the thirteen original colonies and wrote a paper about it.

He invented the Franklin stove, which led to improvement in heating systems.

He built the first electrical battery.

He framed a new theory of electricity in which he pointed to the existence of two types of electrical current—positive and negative. These terms are still used today.

He proved that lightning and electricity are identical.

He invented the lightning rod, a means of avoiding the disastrous effects of lightning, which probably saved many lives and millions of dollars in property. Lightning rods are still used.

He served in the Pennsylvania Assembly for fourteen years and was its most influential member.

He published the first novel ever issued in America—*Pamela*, by Samuel Richardson.

He owned and published the most important newspaper of its time—the *Pennsylvania Gazette*, ancestor of the *Saturday Evening Post.*

He founded the Academy of Pennsylvania, later the University of Pennsylvania.

He advocated inoculation for smallpox many years before it came into general use. He advanced theories about the common cold that are still considered sound.

In the difficult years that preceded the Revolution, he served as a colonial agent in England. During that time he was able to get the Stamp Act repealed. He sacrificed his high position and gave up a brilliant career in America to do this for the sake of his country.

He helped to frame and edit the Declaration of Independence.

He helped to write and accomplish the adoption of the Constitution of the United States, which we continue to live by.

He got money, arms, ammunition, and food for

the American army, while serving as a colonial commissioner in France.

He obtained a sizable loan for the American colonies from the French Government at a time when they needed it most.

He negotiated the treaty of peace between the United States and England at the conclusion of the war.

He advocated the abolition of slavery and published pamphlets on the subject.

These are only the famous things that Ben Franklin did for his country. Nobody knows how many other things he really did in the long years of his busy life. He was never too busy or too important to answer his country's call, or too proud to sacrifice position, fortune, health, and personal happiness in the performance of his duty.

He turned his back on friends and family to join the side of the American colonies. He risked his life to sail to France on the *Reprisal* in the midst of the war. He offered his personal fortune to the Continental Congress and lent and gave money as long as it was needed. He gave his time until the very end of his life. In fact, he withheld nothing from the land he loved.

Ben Franklin said a great many things that are worth remembering, but perhaps he never said anything more important than this: "Where liberty dwells, there is my country."

Index

144

148

149

Landmark Books® Grades 6 and Up